Miracles Fall Like Drops of Rain

Miracles Fall Like Drops of Rain

Inspired Poetry From
A Course in Miracles Workbook for Students

Sandi Christie

Copyright © 2020 by Sandi Christie

All rights reserved. No part of this book may be used or reproduced in any manner whatsoever without written permission of the author. For permissions, contact: verticalperception@mail.com.

All quotes are from *A Course in Miracles*, copyright ©1992, 1999, 2007 by the Foundation for Inner Peace, 448 Ignacio Blvd., #306, Novato, CA 94949, www.acim.org and info@acim.org, used with permission.

ISBN Paperback: 978-1-7360532-0-1
ISBN eBook: 978-1-7360532-1-8

Printed in the United States of America.

Cover and Interior Design: Creative Publishing Book Design

For my mom—
who has always been the light of love in my life,
and for my husband John—
the eternal optimist who lifts me back up.

The poems in this book are meant to correspond to the lessons in the *Workbook for Students* from *A Course in Miracles* but are not meant to be a replacement for the lessons themselves. I have tried to hold the meaning of each lesson as best I could, but no poem can fully encompass the complexity and informative nature of each individual lesson. I recommend reading them with the lessons as you do them, and I hope the poems help keep the lessons' ideas in your mind while you contemplate the meaning. Peace to you on your journey.

About
A Course in Miracles

A Course in Miracles is a self-study spiritual teaching that when understood and practiced can lead to true inner peace: The Peace of God. It does not claim to be the only way to God, but it does claim to hasten the journey getting there. The Course gives the following introduction:

> *"This is a course in miracles. It is a required course. Only the time you take it is voluntary. Free will does not mean that you can establish the curriculum. It means only that you can elect what you want to take at a given time. The course does not aim at teaching the meaning of love, for that is beyond what can be taught. It does aim, however, at removing the blocks to the awareness of love's presence, which is your natural inheritance. The opposite of love is fear, but what is all-encompassing can have no opposite.*
>
> *This course can thereby be summed up very simply in this way:*

Nothing real can be threatened.
Nothing unreal exists.

Herein lies the peace of God." (T-In.1:1-8,2:1-4)

The Preface of *A Course in Miracles* explains how it came about, what it is, and what it says—I invite you to read it if you are not already familiar with the Course. If you do not have a book, you can read it online at the original publisher's (Foundation for Inner Peace) website, www.acim.org.

The Course uses terminology that is found in Eastern teachings as well as terms that sound distinctly Christian. It should be noted that many of these terms are defined in ways that are nontraditional, so an understanding of *The Text* of *A Course in Miracles* is helpful.

Contents

Pledge to God..1

Part I
(Titles with corresponding Lesson numbers)

Only the Love of God Sustains Me (50).................5
I Am the Light (61) 6
Forgiveness Is My Function (62) 7
Your Light Brings Peace (63) 8
Lead Me Not into Temptation (64) 9
God Gave Me Just One Function (65) 10
God Gives Me only Happiness (66) 11
Love Created Me (67) 12
No Grievances (68) 13
The Light of the World Is Inside Me (69) 14
My Salvation Is Within (70) 15
Salvation Will Prevail (71) 16
Holding Grievances Is an Attack on God (72) 18
Darkness Is Not My Will (73) 20
My Will and God's Are One (74) 22
The Light Has Come, the Son Has Risen (75) 23
There are No Laws Except the Laws of God (76) ...24
Miracles Are Your Birthright (77) 25
Let Miracles Restore Your Sight (78) 26

There Is Only One Problem (79) 27
Your Only Problem Has Been Solved (80) 28
Miracles and Vision Go Together (91) 29
Strength Is Light (92) 30
In God, My Sinlessness Is Guaranteed (93) 32
I Am His Son Eternally (94) 33
I Am One Self, Complete and Whole (95) 34
We Find the Peace We Sought to Lose (96) 35
The Truth of You Is Spirit (97) 37
We Side with Truth for Our Salvation (98) 38
Salvation Is Your Only Function Now (99) 39
You Are Essential to God's Plan (100) 40
God's Will of Perfect Happiness We Find (101) 41
The Love of God Has Been Allowed (102) 42
To Fear God Is to Fear Happiness (103) 43
Happiness Is Mine to Find (104) 45
God's Happiness and Peace Are Yours (105) 46
In Stillness I Will Hear the Truth (106) 47
When Truth Has Come (107) 49
Giving and Receiving Are One in Truth (108) 50
We Rest in God (109) 52
I Remain as God Created Me (110) 55
The Unforgiving Mind (121) 57
Forgiveness Offers Everything (122) 59
It's a Day of Love and Gratitude (123) 60
We're One with Him (124) 61
Listen (125) 63
The Giver and Receiver Are the Same (126) 65
There Is No Love but God's Love (127) 66

The World Offers You Nothing (128) 67
There Is a World You Want to Find (129) 69
You Must Decide Which World to View (130) 71
You Cannot Fail to Find the Truth (131) 72
Ideas Leave Not Their Source (132) 74
Don't Value What Is Valueless (133) 76
What Is True Forgiveness? (134) 78
Sickness Has One Attribute (136) 80
You Are Never Healed Alone (137) 82
Heaven Must Be Chosen Consciously (138) 84
Love Is Endless in His Oneness (139) 86
Bring Your Illusions to the Truth (140) 87
Let the Holy Spirit Be the Judge (151) 88
Suffering Is Your Decision (152) 90
Defenselessness Is Strength (153) 92
The Love of God Is All That's True (154) 93
Step Back in Faith and Let Him Lead the Way (155) 94
He Lights My Mind with Happiness (156) 96
Echoes of Eternity (157) 97
The Light We Shine Shines Back on Us (158) 99
Christ's Vision Is the Miracle (159) 101
Salvation Is Acceptance of Your Self (160) 103
Ask Your Brother for His Blessing (161) 105
I Am as God Created Me to Be (162) 107
Death Is Gone, the Mind Is Finally Free (163) 108
The Song of Heaven (164) 109
He Holds You One with All that Is (165) 110
His Gifts are Yours to Give (166) 111
When Dreams of Pain and Death Are Gone (167) 113

Request His Grace and It Is Yours (168) 115
Grace (169) 116
There Is No Cruelty in God (170) 118
The Truth of One Identity (181) 120
The Child in You (182) 121
I Call on God (183) 122
Creation Has One Name (184) 123
The Peace of God (185) 124
It Depends on Me (186) 125
The Grace of God Is in Everyone (187) 126
The Light You Seek Is Still Within (188) 127
Blinded by the Light (189) 128
I Choose the Joy of God (190) 130
I Am the Holy Son (191) 132
I Have a Function (192) 134
All Things Are Forgiveness Lessons (193) 136
Place the Future in His Hands (194) 138
Walk in Gratitude the Way of Love (195) 139
I Crucify Myself (196) 140
It's My Gratitude (197) 142
My Forgiveness Sets Me Free (198) 144
I Am Free (199) 146
The Peace of God (200) 147

Intermission

Forever One, Forevermore (A Spiritual Ode to E.A. Poe) . . 151

Part II

Forgiveness (Part II, #1) 159
I Wait and Listen for Your Voice (221) 160

God Is My Source (222) 161
I Have No Life but God's (223) 162
God Is My Father (224) 163
God's Love Is Blazing in My Mind (225) 164
My Father Awaits My Glad Return (226) 165
My Will Is Yours (227) 166
My Father Knows My Holiness (228) 167
Love I Must Be (229) 168
I Seek His Peace (230) 169
Salvation (Part II, #2) 170
Father, I Seek You (231) 171
A Prayer to God (232) 172
Be My Guide (233) 174
When Dreams of Sin and Guilt Are Gone (234) 175
Your Holiness Is Mine (235) 176
I Rule My Mind (236) 177
I Am as God Created Me (237) 178
His Light Shines in Us (239) 179
Fear Is but Deception (240) 180
The World (Part II, #3) 181
The Holy Instant of Salvation (241) 182
I Will Not Lead My Life Alone (242) 183
Today I Give Up Judgements (243) 184
Your Son Is Safe (244) 185
Father, Your Peace Surrounds Me (245) 186
I Choose to Love Your Son (246) 187
Forgiveness Is the Only Means (247) 188
The Son of God Is One (248) 189
Forgiveness Ends Our Suffering (249) 190

Behold the Son of God (250) 191
Sin (Part II, #4) 192
A Song for God (251) 193
God's Son Is My Identity (252) 194
I Rule My Destiny (253) 195
My Mind Is Finally Still (254) 196
God's Peace Is Mine (255) 197
God Is My Goal (256) 198
No One Serves Opposing Goals (257) 199
Our Goal Is God (258) 200
Sin Is the Thought (259) 201
Let Me Remember You Created Me (260) 203
The Body (Part II, #5) 204
In Him Is Everlasting Peace (261) 205
You Have One Son (262) 206
God's Spirit Is in All Things (263) 207
Salvation's Prayer (264). 208
I Laid My Sins Upon the World (265) 209
Do Not Forget His Name Is Yours (266) 210
In His Peace I Do Rejoice (267) 211
We are Safe in His Identity (268) 212
The Holy Face of Christ I See (269) 213
Christ's Vision Is His Gift to Me (270) 214
Christ (Part II, #6) 215
Christ's Vision Is the Way to You (271) 216
Can Illusions Bring Me Happiness? (272) 217
His Peace Is What I Choose (273) 218
The Voice of Love Is All We Hear (274) 219
Your Healing Voice Protects (275) 220

Have You Heard? (276) 221
The Son of God Cannot Be Bound (277) 222
Dreams of Fear Have Left My Mind (278) 223
Our Freedom Is Already Won (279) 224
I Give Honor to the Son of God (280) 225
The Holy Spirit (Part II, #7) 226
I Must Confess (281) 227
Your Name Is Love and So Is Mine (282) 228
No False Images (283) 229
Thoughts that Hurt Can Be Rejected (284) 230
My Holiness Is Yours (285) 231
There's a Kind of Hush (286) 232
You Are My Only Goal (287) 233
My Brother Is My Savior (288) 234
Let Me Not See a Past that Isn't There (289) 235
My Happiness Is what I See (290) 236
The Real World (Part II, #8) 237
Let Your Memory Return to Me (291) 238
Joy is the Only Outcome (292) 239
Love Remains the Only State (293) 240
The Body Is a Neutral Thing (294) 241
I Use the Eyes of Christ to See (295) 242
The Holy Spirit Needs My Voice (296) 244
Salvation's Creed (297) 245
Eternity with You Is Sure (298). 246
My Holiness Stands Forever Perfect (299). 247
For but an Instant Does This World Endure (300).....248
The Second Coming (Part II, #9) 249
Unless I Judge I Cannot Weep (301) 250

His Light Illuminates the Way (302) 251
Heaven's Son Is Born in Me Today (303) 252
I Can Obscure My Holy Sight (304) 253
The Peace of Christ Is Given to Us (305) 254
We Ask for Only what You Give (306) 255
The End of Conflict (307) 256
The Time Is Now (308) 257
Within Me Is Eternal Innocence (309) 258
This Day I Would Spend with You (310) 259
The Last Judgement (Part II, #10) 260
Father, We Let Your Love Decide (311) 262
I Choose to See No Separation (312) 263
Sin Is Forgiven in His Holy Vision (313) 265
We Use the Present to Be Free (314) 266
Now Our Spirits Are Aligned (315) 267
Every Gift I Give Belongs to Me (316) 268
Where You Lead Is Where I Want to Go (317) 269
In You All Parts are Reconciled (318) 270
My True Self Shares Its Totality (319) 271
The Son of God Is Limitless (320) 272
Creation (Part II, # 11) 273
My Freedom Lies in God (321) 274
The Only Thing I Lose Is Fear (322) 275
You Must Sacrifice Your Suffering (323) 276
We Follow One Who Knows the Way (324) 277
God's Ideas Reflect the Truth (325) 278
I Am Forever Your Effect (326) 279
I Just Call Out Your Name (327) 281
Another Will's Preposterous (328) 282

For Only Your Truth Is True (329) 283
I Choose Not to Hurt Myself Today (330) 284
The Ego (Part II, #12) 285
The Will of God Is One (331) 286
Forgiveness Sets Us Free (332) 287
The Name Remains the Same (333) 288
I Receive Forgiveness by Giving Forgiveness (334) 290
Forgiveness Is a Choice I Make (335) 291
Love Will Open Up the Door (336) 292
My Sinlessness Ensures Me Perfect Peace (337) 293
Your Thoughts Lead Me to Salvation (338) 294
Let's Spend the Day in Fearlessness (339) 295
Our Suffering Is Done (340) 296
Miracles Fall Like Drops of Rain (Part II, #13) 297
Holy Is the Father's Son (341) 299
The Key Is in My Hand (342) 300
Paradise Was Never Lost (343) 301
Today I Learn the Law of Love (344) 302
We Offer Only Miracles Today (345) 303
The Laws of Love Are All I Find (346) 304
I Cast My Hate to the Wind (347) 305
Everlasting Love Surrounds Me (348) 307
Today I Give Up Judgement (349) 308
Spirit Is the Truth of Me (350) 309
Who I Am (Part II, #14) 310
I Make a Choice to See Only what Is True (351) 311
From Judgement Comes All Sorrow (352) 312
My Identity Is Restored in Christ (353) 313
I Am the Christ in Me (354) 314

It's You I Choose Today (355) 315
Sickness Is a Name for Sin (356) 316
Behold His Sinlessness and You Are Healed (357) 317
Let Me Remember (358) 318
The Answer Is Some Form of Peace (359). 319
In Holiness Do We Remain (360) 321
We Can Never Be Apart (361-365) 322
Homeward Bound (Part II, Epilogue). 323

Thank you 325
About the Author 327

Pledge to God

I pledge I love you to the God
That created me exactly as He is.
And to the Holy Spirit—the Voice for God,
All Sons—One with God, indivisible,
In Unity and Oneness and Love.

The following pieces correspond to lessons in the
Workbook for Students of *A Course in Miracles*
and are numbered as such.

PART I

Part I

Only the Love of God Sustains Me
(Inspired by ACIM Lesson 50)

In this world you think you are sustained by everything but God,
Your faith in forms of nothingness whose powers you applaud.
Money, pills and influence; prestige and admiration;
Replacements for the Love of God you hope will bring salvation.

All these things are cherished to ensure you see the body;
Songs of praise sung to the ego can't bring peace to anybody.
Only the Love of God will lift you out of every trial
And raise you high above the dangers that threaten your survival.

Keep faith in your illusions, and they will fail you one by one,
But put your faith in *God in you* and the ego is undone.
Through the *Love of God in you*, all trials are resolved,
And every tribulation and all problems can be solved.

Today's the day we free the mind's belief in all your idols
And let the *Love of God in you* release you from your trials.
Let no foolish thoughts enter and disturb your holy mind;
His truth you'll recognize at last—His peace is what you'll find.

I Am the Light
(Inspired by ACIM Lesson 61)

You are God's Son that He created—
From Him, you can't be separated.
The holy Light of God Himself
Is shared with you and your whole Self.
In spirit you are luminous—
To the ego this is arrogance.
But what is true humility
But accepting your identity
As only what He'd have you be
For now, and in eternity?
Here begins the mind's salvation
That leads away from all temptation,
The answer to the world's illusions,
Releasing you from your confusion.
The light within shines very bright—
Allow it to restore your sight
And shine it on the world you see—
Accept your holy destiny.

Part I

Forgiveness Is My Function
(Inspired by ACIM Lesson 62)

In your forgiveness lies salvation;
Your memory unfurled,
Forgiveness is the demonstration—
Your light lights up the world.

Forgiveness is a gift you give
To no one but yourself,
And every time that you forgive
You acknowledge your true Self.

Every time that you attack
You call upon your weakness;
The strength of Christ you do not lack,
When you allow forgiveness.

Happiness I will achieve
When I fulfill my function;
The truth of God I will believe
As I pass this crucial junction.

Your Light Brings Peace
(Inspired by ACIM Lesson 63)

Within you is the power to bring peace—
Is there a greater gift that you could give,
That leads to joy and suffering's release,
And happiness each time that you forgive?

How fortunate are you who recognize,
The truth forgiveness brings into your mind—
The light of love that lifts the dark disguise,
With eyes that see, no longer are they blind.

The world you see is waiting to be blessed—
Do not forget the function that you hold.
Forgiveness given is no small request;
The light it brings is something to behold.

The light you bring brings peace to every mind,
And now you see, your Self is what you find.

Part I

Lead Me Not into Temptation
(Inspired by ACIM Lesson 64)

Lead me not into temptation,
Let me recognize salvation,
Give up painful lamentations
For amazing revelations.

The purpose of the world obscures
The hidden spirit that still is pure.
God's Love within us will endure—
When we forgive, it is the cure.

The body's eyes see but illusions—
Reflections of the mind's delusions,
And all the ego's dark intrusions
Will only leave the mind in ruins.

Fulfill your function and you will light
The world before you very bright.
Think you do not have God's might?
You have the Holy Spirit's sight.

Fulfill your function and you will see
Just how happy you can be.
Give up all your complexity,
And you will see your mind as free.

God Gave Me Just One Function
(Inspired from ACIM Lesson 65)

Acceptance of salvation is but all you need to do,
A commitment made to God that accepts His Love is true.
God's promise is salvation so that you might find your way
Past dark illusions in your mind that seem to lead astray.

You have no other function here, nothing else you have to do;
All other goals that you invent are idols you pursue.
This is the only way in which your mind will be at peace,
Escape from dreams of conflict and allowing pain to cease.

Part I

God Gives Me Only Happiness
(Inspired by ACIM Lesson 66)

When you fulfill your function true,
Happiness will come to you.
You don't see the connection yet—
The ego wants you to forget.
There is a battle that is fought
Between Spirit and the ego's thought.
The ego's will is to attack;
The Holy Spirit does not react.
He knows what brings you happiness;
Battles here are meaningless.
Spirit knows about your function—
Don't accept ego's dysfunction.
Happiness, it then must be,
The function He has given me.

Love Created Me
(Inspired by ACIM Lesson 67)

Holiness created you holy;
Kindness created you kind;
How can the Son be unholy
When God is the Light in your mind?

Love created you like Itself;
Truth created you true;
It's time that you remind yourself,
This Self must be in you.

Part I

No Grievances
(Inspired by ACIM Lesson 68)

You were created by Love like Itself
And can't hold a grievance and know your Self,
Or the body is seen as the vision is blind,
And the ego now rules, in charge of your mind.
You now seem to be split off from your Source,
A body condemned with little recourse.

Shut off from your Self, your Self seems to sleep,
Weaving illusions the mind wants to keep.
Your image of God has been redefined
As fearful and angry and very inclined
To punish his Son for the dreams he has built,
As grievances held keep his mind full of guilt.

It's only when you let grievances cease,
That you will finally find your peace.
Would you let them all go if you knew this were so?
Perhaps you don't think you can let them all go.
Peace is a matter of motivation—
Love holds no grievances: it's your salvation.

The Light of the World Is Inside Me
(Inspired by ACIM Lesson 69)

The light of the world is inside me;
The light of the world is in you,
Yet darkness is our reality—
Grievances distort our view.

Everyone stands in darkness now;
Dark heavy clouds surround us.
The veil of darkness does not allow
The vision of light that's within us.

The clouds seem to be our reality—
We don't know that we can go through them.
They seem to be all there is to see,
But we will attempt to move past them.

Today we will try to reach to the light,
And reach past the veil of darkness.
With determination we call on His might
To lift us out of our madness.

Part I

My Salvation Is Within
(Inspired by ACIM Lesson 70)

My Salvation comes from me—
It's where God put the remedy;
It stands with guilt inside my mind
That I might choose which one to find.

Nothing outside myself can save me;
Nothing outside myself can hurt me;
Nothing outside myself brings peace
Or the love that cannot cease.

All the things that bring me pleasure
Are substitutes for God's own treasure.
They only lead into temptation
To believe they bring salvation.

Sickness seen in anybody
Is of the mind, not of the body.
Sickness makes us all unhappy—
God's will for us is to be happy.

We try to reach the light within,
Where our salvation has always been.
My salvation comes from me—
I will not look outside of me.

Salvation Will Prevail
(Inspired by ACIM Lesson 71)

The ego's plan for your salvation
Is preposterous, it's true;
Its plan results in your damnation,
And believe in it, you do.

If someone acted differently,
If some event were changed—
Then you would have serenity,
And then you would be saved.

Now the source of your salvation
Is perceived outside yourself.
Each grievance held—a declaration—
All must change except yourself.

The fruitless search will never bless
Because illusions must address
That joy is found in someone else;
Another event will yield success.

And so, the ego's plan you see
Is "Seek but do not find."
What else could surely guarantee
Your vision will stay blind?

Part I

God promises you will succeed
By following His direction;
His plan for you will not mislead
If you make the right selection.

His plan will work, His plan will save—
Its outcome cannot fail.
Seek only but the plan He gave,
And salvation will prevail.

Holding Grievances Is an Attack on God
(Inspired by ACIM Lesson 72)

The ego's plan for your salvation opposes God's own plan;
Its attacks now seem to give to God the attributes of man.
The ego's fundamental wish is to be God's replacement;
It is that wish that traps the mind into a flesh encasement.

The limitations that a body would impose are obvious,
But the grievances you hold are for what the *body* does.
You are not dealing here with what the person really is,
For God created him as spirit, and that spirit's just like His.

Every grievance that you hold insists the body's real
And condemns the body for it without hope of an appeal.
It declares that his salvation must be death, and it projects
This attack back onto God and holds Him responsible for it.

If God's Son is just a body, God must be a body too,
And His plan for our salvation is the hell He leads us to.
Whatever could He offer us but pain, disease and death?
He must live only to punish us before stealing our last breath.

For such is the insanity of all the world you see,
The body now your savior as the ego would have it be.
But while you hold the body as your concept of yourself,
Every grievance that you hold is merely held against your Self.

Part I

The glory of the body but attacks your own salvation,
Holding grievances against Him and His innocent creation.
You cannot hear the Voice of truth and welcome it as friend,
As the body as your savior takes His place for you instead.

Your upside-down perception has destroyed your peace of mind—
You seem locked inside a body and the truth you cannot find,
But the light of truth is in us where it was placed by God—
The spirit is the truth of you; the body is a fraud.

Darkness Is Not My Will
(Inspired by ACIM Lesson 73)

The will you share with God
Has all the power of creation,
But wishes that the ego lauds
Are but dreams of separation.
They make a world of your illusions
That has a very strong appeal,
But they're still the mind's delusions—
They make nothing that is real.

The ego's idle wishes
Did give rise to what you see,
And the ego's need for grievances
Maintains it endlessly.
It peoples it with figures seen
That now seem to attack you,
And the figures seen now seem
To hide the light of what is true.

Your real will is lost to you
In this world where guilt is traded
Back and forth, it does accrue,
Every grievance celebrated.
Could such a world have come about
By a Will that's shared as One?
A world of fear and pain and doubt,
And death for everyone?

Part I

The vision of the world you see
Reflects what is within.
Your grievances cloud what you see—
A now darkened world of sin.
Forgiveness clears your darkened sight
And reasserts your will,
And lets you see a world of light
Salvation has fulfilled.

My Will and God's Are One
(Inspired by ACIM Lesson 74)

I am only an expression—
God's own glorious extension;
There's no other truth but this,
So I have no goal but His.

My mind is now at peace,
Thoughts of conflict all released,
There's no longer a confusion
From erroneous illusions.

There is no will but God's—
Dreams of hate have been outlawed,
There is nothing to disturb me—
Nothing outside can perturb me.

Conflict thoughts are meaningless,
And replaced with forgiveness.
My will and God's are One,
And God wills peace for His own Son.

Part I

The Light Has Come, the Son Has Risen
(Inspired by ACIM Lesson 75)

The light has come, there's no division—
We use the Holy Spirit's vision,
No shadows darken what we see,
We celebrate most happily—
A joyous world we now envision.

The light that shines has left no sin—
Today, the time of light begins,
And all we see has been made free—
The light has come.

No longer blind, His Sight is given—
The world we see has been forgiven,
Our mind has now been healed completely,
Reflecting Heaven in all we see.
We now rejoice, the Son has risen—
The light has come.

There Are No Laws Except the Laws of God
(Inspired by ACIM Lesson 76)

There are no laws except the laws of God—
The laws you made to govern are a fraud,
All that you made opposes God's own Will,
And not a thing the body seeks fulfills.

The laws of God can never be replaced;
His memory can never be erased.
The laws you made keep you in custody;
The laws of God will always set you free.

God's laws forever give and never take;
He knows that what you made was a mistake.
Each law held in the ego's claim to fame
Can never save but damns in Heaven's name.

There are no laws except the laws of God—
The logic that the ego lends is flawed;
The mind that understands this will applaud—
There are no laws except the laws of God.

Part I

Miracles Are Your Birthright
(Inspired by ACIM Lesson 77)

Miracles are your own birthright—
You receive them in God's holy Light.
Salvation declares you are His Son;
Miracles show that you are One.

They don't depend upon illusions—
They are natural conclusions,
Inherent in the truth of you,
Held by the laws that God imbues.

Miracles are your given right—
They will adjust your earthly sight,
And release you from the world you made,
Where dreams of pain and death invade.

I am entitled to miracles—
Their request is nothing mystical.
There is no room for disbelief;
Forgiveness is my leitmotif.

Let Miracles Restore Your Sight
(Inspired by ACIM Lesson 78)

Every decision that you make,
You choose the light or see mistakes;
Each grievance stands like a shield of hate,
And miracles will have to wait.

We must reverse the way you see,
For sight must stop before it sees.
We will not hold a shield of hate;
We'll lay it down and change our fate.

The Son appears in shining light,
Where grievances used to block the sight;
It lifts you high to see God's Son,
And lets the darkness be undone.

We look toward truth, away from fear,
And let all grievances disappear.
Let your mind be shown the light,
And miracles restore your sight.

Part I

There Is Only One Problem
(Inspired by ACIM Lesson 79)

A problem can't be solved if you do not know what it is;
Even when the problem's solved, you will not realize it is.
The world has but one problem, and that problem has been solved,
But if you cannot see the problem, you don't know it's been resolved.

Everyone has special problems, yet they're really all the same,
And this must now be recognized for the solution to be claimed.
Who can know the problem's solved if you think it's something else,
For even with the answer, you can't see its relevance.

There's no end to all the problems that seem to cloud your eyes,
And as each one is settled then another does arise.
No one could solve all problems that the world appears to hold—
You've been dealt a hand you cannot win, and now it's time to fold.

Yet all of this complexity is a smokescreen to conceal
That you have only one problem, and this truth is very real.
Separation is your problem, no matter what form it takes,
And until you recognize this, it's your joy that is at stake.

Your Only Problem has been Solved
(Inspired by ACIM Lesson 80)

Your only problem has been solved—
It's this we recognize;
With this, all others are resolved,
We've opened up our eyes.

Therefore, you must be at peace—
This is your salvation,
Freed from war's accepted lease,
In happy jubilation.

Deception has been laid aside,
And seen in holy light;
The law of One has been applied—
The world is seen aright.

We claim the peace that must be ours—
God's answer has not failed.
We have accepted what we are;
The train has not derailed.

Part I

Miracles and Vision Go Together
(Inspired by ACIM Lesson 91)

It is important to remember,
Miracles and vision go together.
The miracle is always there—
When you're in the dark, you're unaware.

From where the darkness still is seen,
The miracle remains unseen;
The light that's there is not received,
For only darkness is perceived.

You know the body's eyes can see,
But they do not see reality.
Your vision needs to be reversed,
And what you see cannot be cursed.

Your belief in what you think you are
Must be undone and left afar;
Body belief calls for correction—
It calls for spiritual resurrection.

Strength Is Light
(Inspired by ACIM Lesson 92)

Strength is light—
It is God's might,
His holy Sight
And your birth right.
His strength denies
Where weakness lies,
And the body's eyes
Only disguise.
His strength in you
Is the light in you;
His holy view
Must now come through.
It is weakness
That looks in darkness,
A loveless witness
Without forgiveness.
Its darkness grows;
Its hatred flows;
Attack it chose;
Judgement it knows.
The strength of light
Will never fight;
It shares its sight
In love's delight.
Strength and light

Part I

Unite in you;
It guides us true,
Embracing you.
Joy has begun;
Darkness is done;
And now the Son
Can stand as One.

In God, My Sinlessness Is Guaranteed
(Inspired by ACIM Lesson 93)

You think you are the home of darkness and of sin,
And now you are afraid of all the evil that's within.
You think if what is true about yourself were now revealed,
You'd be struck with horror so severe it couldn't be concealed.

These things that you believe in are really based on nothing;
The mistakes made within dreams simply have no real meaning.
Fantasies and savage dreams and idols made of dust—
Such idle thoughts are meaningless, and it's in these things you trust.

These weird beliefs you seem to have do not uphold God's Will;
You should be overjoyed to know that what you are is not evil.
You are still as God created you, as holy and as pure;
His Light and joy and peace abide in you, and that's for sure.

This self you made is not the Son of God and is not real;
The effects of all it seems to do or think have been repealed.
Your sinlessness is guaranteed by God, and He proclaims
What He creates is just like Him and forever stays the same.

    Repeat this truth right now and try to see:

Light and joy and peace abide in me,
In God, my sinlessness is guaranteed.
The mind that understands this will be freed,
In God, my sinlessness is guaranteed.

Part I

I Am His Son Eternally
(Inspired by Lesson 94)

I am as God created me—
The key to my salvation.
I am His Son eternally.

The ego's gone entirely—
Powerless is all temptation.
I am as God created me.

Restored is all my sanity—
His glorious One Creation!
I am His Son eternally.

I walk in perfect certainty—
In fearless ambulation.
I am as God created me.

His Light burns bright inside of me—
Darkness fades, Illumination!
I am His Son eternally.

I remain throughout eternity—
In joyous celebration!
I am as God created me;
I am His Son eternally.

I Am One Self, Complete and Whole
(Inspired by ACIM Lesson 95)

You are One within yourself,
And you are One with Him,
Yet you do not accept your Self,
And can't see the light within.

You believe you are a body,
Weak and sinful, full of pain,
A most outrageous parody
Of the union God ordained.

A self that's now divided
Into many warring parts,
Erratic and misguided,
A separate thing that lives apart.

And now the God you pray to
Seems not to hear your prayers,
For He must be insane like you—
Blind and deaf, He does not care.

Let all these errors go away;
See the truth of what they are;
These thoughts have led your mind astray,
Keeping peace and joy afar.

I am One Self, complete and whole,
United with my brother;
This holy Self that I extol
Still remains One with the Father.

Part I

We Find the Peace We Sought to Lose
(Inspired by ACIM Lesson 96)

You experience yourself as two, although you are one Self—
You're good and evil, mind and body, this thing and something else.
This sense of being split leads to a state of constant conflict,
And leads to mad attempts to try to reconcile the opposites.

Truth and illusion can't be reconciled, no matter how you try;
Good and evil have no meeting place and can't be rectified.
The self you made can never be your Self—the Self is One;
A mind and body cannot both exist within God's Son.

Spirit makes use of mind as means to find its Self-expression,
And the mind which serves the Spirit is at peace in love's reflection.
Yet mind can see itself divorced from Spirit, in a body,
And confuse that body with itself with the mind in custody.

The mind apart from Spirit cannot think, its Source denied—
It sees itself as helpless, limited and petrified.
Dissociated from its function, it thinks it's all alone,
Lost upon a battleground, attacked by armies, on its own.

Who can resolve the conflicts that this senseless dream presents?
Salvation can't make illusions real, despite the mind's pretense,
Nor solve a problem that does not exist in God's reality,
But you can choose God's plan for you, and let it set you free.

Your Self retains Its Thoughts, and they remain within your mind;
The Holy Spirit holds them there, awaiting you to find.
Salvation comes from your own Self; Its Thoughts are yours to use—
Claim them as your own, and you've found the peace you sought
    to lose.

Part I

The Truth of You Is Spirit
(Inspired by ACIM Lesson 97)

The truth of you is spirit—
There's no other truth than this,
It releases mind from conflict
And unites your mind with His.
It absolves you of your madness
Of a split identity,
For there can be no sadness
In God's perfect Unity.

We state the truth about yourself—
God's Son resides in you;
Spirit is your One-True-Self—
God shares Himself with you.
We try to bring reality
Still closer to your mind,
By giving up insanity
And leaving it behind.

What I am is purely spirit—
This is my given role,
I'm free of every limit,
Safe, and healed and whole.
The Holy Spirit takes my gifts
And multiplies each one;
He blesses and returns each gift—
They're shared with everyone.

We Side with Truth for Our Salvation
(Inspired by ACIM Lesson 98)

It is a day of dedication
To the ego's eradication;
We side with truth for our salvation,
Without a hint of vacillation.

All doubts are laid aside today—
We take our stand without delay,
Not one mistake stands in our way,
All of our sins have washed away.

We have a purpose to fulfill;
Without judgement, our minds are still,
For we will never rest until
Our only function can be filled.

The guiltless know their safety's sure,
For they are safe and now secure.
They rest in certainty so pure—
The light within can't be obscured.

All who took the stand we take
Will offer every gain they make;
God's Love is pure and can't forsake
His holy Son who's now awake.

Part I

Salvation Is Your Only Function Now
(Inspired by ACIM Lesson 99)

Salvation and forgiveness are the same—
They both imply that you forgot your name.
It seems a thing impossible occurred,
Apart or different from His holy Word.

Truth and illusions both are equal now,
And all illusions must be disavowed;
Salvation now becomes the borderland
Between the truth and dreams that are at hand.

The mind that sees illusions thinks them real;
In worlds of dreams, they have a strong appeal,
And yet they are not real because the mind
That thought them is apart from God and blind.

What but a Thought of God could heal the Son,
Overlooking that which was never done,
And forgetting sins that were never real,
In a separate mind where truth has been concealed.

The Holy Spirit looks on what you see—
Sin and pain and death and insanity—
Yet does He know one thing must still be true—
God still is Love and dreams must be seen through.

This is the Thought that saves and that forgives;
The function that It has is what It gives.
Salvation is your only function now—
God still is Love, and this must be allowed.

You Are Essential to God's Plan
(Inspired by ACIM Lesson 100)

You are essential to God's plan,
Given to you when time began;
Your joy must be complete to know
The light within lets sorrow go.

God's messengers are everywhere;
Their inner joy heals all despair;
They're proof God's Will is happiness
For all who choose God's Will as theirs.

We will not be depressed today
By choosing a different part to play;
We will accept but one assignment
With the joy of mind's alignment.

Joy is your only function here—
If you are sad or live in fear,
Then all the world's deprived of joy
And happiness that God employs.

God's holy messenger you are—
Your joy heals all those near and far;
To everything you look upon,
His peace is shared with everyone.

You are not asked to sacrifice—
You're asked to open up your eyes.
You are essential to God's plan—
Salvation of the mind of man.

Part I

God's Will of Perfect Happiness We Find
(Inspired by ACIM Lesson 101)

You still believe God asks for suffering
As punishment for every sin you bring,
And so you must believe that sin is real,
And that it warrants death without appeal.

If sin is real, then punishment is just—
The Son cannot be seen without disgust,
And punishment can never be escaped,
For the sinful ask for death as their own fate.

If sin is real, salvation must be pain,
The cost of sin where illusions still remain.
Salvation must be feared for it will kill—
From a vengeful God whose wrath cannot be filled.

Who would seek such savage punishment?
And live in fear from its own banishment?
If sin is real, salvation must be feared—
For God is wrath, and love has disappeared.

Today we will remember sin's not real;
We let it go and allow the mind to heal.
Accept Atonement with an open mind—
God's Will of perfect happiness we find.

The Love of God Has Been Allowed
(Inspired by ACIM Lesson 102)

I choose to give up suffering—
It does not buy me anything;
I know now that it makes no sense—
It but attacks my innocence.

Every pain is purposeless,
Without a cause and powerless;
It cannot purchase anything—
It offers only suffering.

I'm free today to join God's Will—
His function for me I will fill.
His Will for me is happiness,
And what He Wills, I will possess.

I share God's Will for happiness,
Accepted now without duress;
It is my only function now—
The Love of God has been allowed.

Part I

To Fear God Is to Fear Happiness
(Inspired by ACIM Lesson 103)

Happiness is
Love's attribute—
It's limitless
Without refute.
It's everywhere—
There are no gaps,
And joy is there—
They overlap.
Yet can the mind
Deny it's so,
Disinclined
To let dreams go.
It redefines
The love it is
As not Divine
And limited.
This strange belief
Would limit joy—
An angry thief
The mind employs,
Introducing
Opposition,
Circumventing
God's position.
God is now fear

Instead of Love—
Joy disappears
In heartache's trove.
Yet nonetheless,
God, being Love,
Is happiness
Without fear of.
To fear Him is
To be afraid
Of happiness
That you mislaid.

Part I

Happiness Is Mine to Find
(Inspired by ACIM Lesson 104)

There is an altar in my mind
With gifts of God I cannot find.
The joy He gives can't be located
When the altar's desecrated.

This altar has no open space,
For self-made gifts have now been placed—
Anxiety, despair and pain,
Hate and judgement are what reign.

The altar to the body rules;
We do not see we've become fools,
And yet, His gifts remain inside,
Found when we lay ours aside.

I seek the gifts He's given me;
Happiness is my destiny,
Joy and peace my inheritance,
Received from Him without expense.

The conflicts of the world released—
I seek only to find His peace,
And clear a place within my mind,
And happiness is mine to find.

God's Happiness and Peace Are Yours
(Inspired by ACIM Lesson 105)

God's happiness and peace are yours; He shares it all with you.
They are not like the gifts of man, where the giver seems to lose,
And the taker made richer by his loss in bargains made with guilt,
For this could only seem to be in the dreams that you have built.

It's impossible that one can gain because another loses,
As this implies a limit and lack in separation's ruses.
For giving's now a source of fear and something you should shun,
But giving's the means where you receive—it's shared with everyone.

God's gifts will never lessen when they are given away—
Accept God's peace and joy, and you will learn a different way
Of looking at a gift, where when they're given, they increase,
Intensifying the joy you feel and extending Heaven's peace.

True giving is creation— it extends the limitless
To the unlimited, and eternity to timelessness.
It adds all to all that is complete without terms of adding more,
For more implies that it was somehow incomplete before.

Accept God's peace and joy as yours; let Him define completion;
The Father shares all with the Son without any depletion.
The Father cannot give through loss, and you are just like Him;
Receive His gift of joy today, and you share your gift with Him.

Part I

In Stillness I Will Hear the Truth
(Inspired by ACIM Lesson 106)

Lay the ego's voice aside—
It offers only nothing;
Listen where His Voice resides
And to the truth He brings.

Hear the mighty Voice of truth,
In quiet certainty;
Silence voices of untruth,
Accept your destiny.

Be still today and listen—
Hear your Father speak to you
In the quiet space within
Where His Spirit speaks what's true.

Be not afraid to circumvent
The voices of the world,
Past all things that represent
The world where darkness rules.

Hear Him and be silent,
For He would speak to you;
Allow His pledge that's ancient
To be kept for all of you.

Listen to the Word which lifts
The veil from your eyes,
Reaching all those set adrift
Lost under angry skies.

Miracles Fall Like Drops of Rain

Listen close and you will hear
A Voice which will resound,
Through the world from your own ear
To everyone around.

And everything you give away
Remains with you forever;
A lesson has been learned today—
We are His messengers.

Part I

When Truth Has Come
(Inspired by ACIM Lesson 107)

When truth has come, all errors seen now simply disappear,
Vanishing without a trace, and with it every fear.
Fading into nothingness, returning whence they came,
From dust to dust they come and go, for only truth remains.

When truth has come, there's nothing that can interrupt your peace,
For you are loved and safe and sure, and this can never cease.
Without illusions, there's no fear and no one can attack,
All pain is gone forever, and there can never be a lack.

When truth has come, it does not stay a while and disappear;
It does not shift and change its form to go and reappear.
It stays exactly as it was, fulfilling every need,
Correcting errors in your mind, and with that, it is freed.

When truth has come, it harbors gifts of perfect constancy,
Of love which does not falter in the face of pain's decree.
The truth will lift you far beyond illusions and ensure
That the truth needs no defenses as it's perfectly secure.

When truth has come, it does not hide—it stands in open light;
No one can seek it truly without setting mind alight.
You were not meant to suffer, and you were not meant to die;
Your Father wills these dreams be gone; His truth corrects the lies.

Giving and Receiving Are One in Truth
(Inspired by ACIM Lesson 108)

What is light but resolution—
The joy of mind's own restitution;
All conflict thoughts have been released—
It is the light that's born of peace.

It is true light that makes true vision,
A state of mind that ends division;
A mind so whole that when darkness calls,
It cannot be perceived at all.

What is the same is seen as One;
Separation is undone.
What's not the same is out of sight,
And can't be seen in the true light.

This light can show no opposite;
It brings your peace of mind with it
To share with other minds like yours,
Reminding we are One with Source.

What God created like Himself,
Is still at One with His true Self,
Forever in a state of grace,
Where there can be no second place.

Here, it's understood that giving
Is not different from receiving.
Different aspects of One Thought,
When extended, ties the knot.

Part I

To give and to receive are one,
In truth for you and everyone.
We offer peace to all, and thus
We see that peace returned to us.

We Rest in God
(Inspired by ACIM Lesson 109)

We ask for only rest today and peace that stills a nation—
    I rest in God
We ask for only happiness that lasts for the duration—
    I rest in God
In the midst of turmoil, of danger and of sorrow,
We have the thought that answers and brings hope for our tomorrows.
    I rest in God, I rest in God.

This thought will bring His peace to you and still your troubled mind—
    I rest in God
And with it safety and His happiness you'll find—
    I rest in God
This thought has all the power now to wake you from your sleep,
Here is the end of suffering that all who came here seem to reap.
    I rest in God, I rest in God.

This thought will carry you through thunder storms and strife—
    I rest in God
Past misery and loss and death to everlasting life—
    I rest in God
Onward to the certainty of God and all that's real,
There's no problem it can't solve, no pain it cannot heal.
    I rest in God, I rest in God.

Part I

While the world is torn by winds of hate, you're undisturbed—
> I rest in God

Appearances cannot intrude on you, you're unconcerned—
> I rest in God

You call to all to join you in your rest and they will hear
The Voice of God that comes through when the ego disappears.
> I rest in God, I rest in God.

In Him you have no cares, no pain and no anxiety—
> I rest in God

There's no past regrets or future fears in eternity—
> I rest in God

In timelessness you rest while time goes by without a call
For your peace and rest can never change in any way at all.
> I rest in God, I rest in God.

Close your eyes and sink into the stillness peace allows—
> I rest in God

And be thankful no more fearful dreams will come at all for now—
> I rest in God

A bird with broken wings now sings, a tired mind made glad,
A stream long dry now flows again, the world's no longer sad.
> I rest in God, I rest in God.

Miracles Fall Like Drops of Rain

You rest within the peace of God, quiet and unafraid—
    I rest in God
Each brother comes to take his rest with you, his lilies laid—
    I rest in God
We rest together here, for thus our rest is made complete,
And all the peace we give today, we have by now received.
    I rest in God, I rest in God.

Part I

I Remain as God Created Me
(Inspired by ACIM Lesson 110)

I am as God created me—
This is the truth that sets me free.
Reality has never changed;
Heaven was not rearranged;
Pain and death do not exist;
No notes in Heaven's song were missed.

This is the thought that heals my mind—
His perfect vision I will find;
All mistakes will be erased
Throughout time in any place.
The past now healed, the future free,
Escape from time's insanity.

If you remain as God created
Your spirit can't be separated—
Death is not life's substitute;
Fear is not love's attribute;
What you see cannot be true—
You're still as God created you.

You need no thought but just this one,
And in this thought the past's undone;
The present saved to now extend
Timelessness that cannot end.
Your mind is not apart from His;
Today's idea is limitless.

Miracles Fall Like Drops of Rain

I am as God created me—
The Word of God that sets me free,
The key that opens up the gate,
Unlocking Heaven as my fate.
The peace of God my destiny,
Forever in eternity.

Part I

The Unforgiving Mind
(Inspired by ACIM Lesson 121)

The unforgiving mind is full of fear and pain;
It offers love no room to ever be attained.
There is no place where it can spread its wings and soar
Above the turmoil of the world outside the door.

The unforgiving mind is sad and without hope;
It suffers in its pain while walking a tightrope.
It peers about in darkness never seeing as it's blind,
Certain of the danger up ahead and just behind.

The unforgiving mind is torn with guilt and doubt,
Confused about itself and all it sees about,
Afraid to go ahead, and yet afraid to stay,
Afraid to sleep or wake, afraid to fade away.

The unforgiving mind is afraid of every sound,
Yet more afraid of stillness if the truth should come around.
Terrified of darkness but more fearful of the light,
Afraid of its damnation in a state of fight or flight.

The unforgiving mind sees no mistakes, just sin,
Afraid of darkness in the world, afraid of what's within.
It shrieks as it sees its own projections rising to attack,
And dreams of future misery which offers only lack.

The unforgiving mind condemns the world it sees,
And does not see it has condemned itself to insanity.
It sees its judgement of the world as irreversible;
It thinks its judgement is correct; it's never merciful.

Each unforgiving mind is an opportunity,
To teach your mind how to forgive by seeing Unity.
The Holy Spirit's Voice will lead— we use His holy Sight
To look past the mind's container and find the hidden light.

Part I

Forgiveness Offers Everything
(Inspired by ACIM Lesson 122)

Forgiveness offers everything—
The peace of God is all I see;
The end of all my suffering.

Eternal joy is what it brings—
A sense of worth and certainty.
Forgiveness offers everything.

Gifts of God that keep on giving,
Dead thoughts have cleared my memory—
The end of all my suffering.

Angry eyes are now forgiving;
The answer's here for all to see—
Forgiveness offers everything.

Salvation is the plan He brings—
It stands before you changelessly,
The end of all your suffering.

The gift of light is what I bring,
Sharing deep tranquility.
Forgiveness offers everything—
The end of all our suffering.

It's a Day of Love and Gratitude
(Inspired by ACIM Lesson 123)

It's a day of love and gratitude
For He has not abandoned you
And left you here all on your own
To wander in the dark alone.
Be grateful now, for He has saved
You from the self you thought you made.

What you thought you left behind
Was never lost, just out of mind.
His Love forever shines on you
Without a change—it's always true.
Give thanks as well that your true Self
Is as changeless as Himself.

In gratitude we lift our hearts
As now we know we're not apart.
Our thankful eyes will not despair—
We see His Light shine everywhere.
We celebrate our destiny
And share in One Identity.

Part I

We're One with Him
(Inspired by ACIM Lesson 124)

We now give thanks for our Identity—
Our home is safe, protection guaranteed,
And God's own strength's available to us,
For God Himself goes everywhere in us.

Now all we touch takes on a shining light,
That heals and blesses every single fright.
How easily do errors disappear,
For death is gone, eternal life is here.

His Light reflected in our minds will soothe;
Our shining footprints point the way to truth.
He walks beside us in the world a while;
We go our way rejoicing with a smile.

All those who come to follow us will see
The way before them for the light that we
Bring with us stays behind yet still remains
Around us on the path that He sustains.

What we receive is our eternal gift,
Shared wholly with the mind that seemed to split,
He loves each part completely equally;
The split we see is not reality.

We're One with Him; we feel Him in our hearts;
Our minds contain His Thoughts; we're not apart.
His loveliness is all we see today;
Appearances of pain have gone away.

Miracles Fall Like Drops of Rain

No miracle can ever be denied
To those who know they're One with God inside.
Their thoughts have power, ending suffering;
Minds joined as One are now enlightening.

We join in this awareness as we say
That we are One with God Himself today;
For in these words we're saved, and we are healed,
The truth of One's accepted as ideal.

Part I

Listen
(Inspired by ACIM Lesson 125)

Listen
In the quiet of the day
Listen
To what the Father has to say
Quiet
In the stillness of your mind
Quiet
It is His peace that you will find
Freedom
You are forever free
Freedom
As He created you to be
Judgement
Of the Son the world has laid
Judgement
Has been forever stayed
Stillness
We will hear His Voice today
Stillness
With our thoughts out of the way
Hear now
Only His holy Word
Hear now
To be spread across the world
Altar

Miracles Fall Like Drops of Rain

The quiet place inside
Altar
Where the Father does abide
Listen
Let Him give His Word to you
Listen
He does not hide Himself from you
Madness
You have wandered off in dreams
Madness
It is His truth that will redeem
Silence
When the mind is finally still
Silence
An open space His Love will fill.

Part I

The Giver and the Receiver Are the Same
(Inspired by ACIM Lesson 126)

All that I give is given to myself—
The only truth's the truth of my own Self.
I share this truth with everyone I see,
When all I see is Unified with me.

And if I see a body that has sinned,
The truth of Oneness in my mind has dimmed.
Illusions in my mind have now replaced,
The memory of Christ's innocent face.

Forgiveness does not pardon someone's sins—
It does not see outside; it looks within.
It offers a correction for the mind,
And it accepts Atonement for mankind.

The giver and receiver are the same—
Now Unified, their spirit shares One Name.
The bodies that we see were never real;
The truth of spirit is the real deal.

There Is No Love but God's Love
(Inspired by ACIM Lesson 127)

Perhaps you think that different kinds of love are possible,
A little here, a lot more there, for her there's none at all.
But real love has no distinctions, it does not have degrees;
There are no conditions it can hold and no divergencies.

Love's meaning is obscure to all who think that love can change,
Bestowed on one more worthy while from others it's estranged,
And think that you can love sometimes and let it turn to hate—
Is not to know of love at all, and this you demonstrate.

God is Love, and Love is One— its meaning lies in Oneness;
It must elude the mind that does not think in terms of wholeness.
There is no love but God's Love, and all of Love is His;
Love's meaning is your own for what you are is what He is.

There is no love but God's Love— it's unaltering and sure,
For what God is— is Love itself, a Love completely pure.
It shares Its Love with Its Whole Self; It shares it with the Son;
Love is God's only principle, and it holds the world as One.

No law the world obeys can ever help you grasp Love's meaning;
The world's beliefs were meant to hide the truth and keep you dreaming.
But God Himself has placed a spark of truth within your mind,
So when false beliefs are given up, His truth you now can find.

Part I

The World Offers You Nothing
(Inspired by ACIM Lesson 128)

The truth of you is spirit—
And the spirit has no needs;
It soars without a limit
In a mind that's finally freed
Of every form of misery
And storm clouds of despair,
For there can be no injury
In the mind that's now aware.

The world you see holds nothing—
It's a chain around your neck,
A gift of endless suffering
On a ship that's going to wreck.
And all the things you value
Forge the chains that tie you down—
You must accept this thought as true
If you would fly above the ground.

All the things you seek to make
Your value greater in your sight
Now limit you and do forsake
The strength of Self and hide the light.
Body thoughts are but temptation
To believe there's something here
That will offer you salvation
While the truth does disappear.

Miracles Fall Like Drops of Rain

There is nothing here to cherish—
Nothing here is worth the pain
In dreams that are nightmarish,
Where suffering does reign.
So rise above the world you see,
Release your mind from chains,
Restoring it to sanity,
Where only love remains.

Part I

There Is a World You Want to Find
(Inspired by ACIM Lesson 129)

The world you see is merciless,
Unconcerned with you and hateful;
Quick to avenge and pitiless,
A world that is unstable.
Here, no lasting love is found,
For real love does not exist here
On the field of time's battleground,
Where good things disappear.

Is it a loss to find instead
A world where losing is impossible?
A place where fear can never tread,
And love is inexhaustible?
Here true love endures forever,
As hate does not exist.
Vengeance has no door to enter,
And peacefulness persists.

The love, the peace and joy you need
Can never have an ending;
In Him forever guaranteed
To stay the same without relenting.
God's language remains unspoken,
And yet it's surely understood,
For what is One cannot be broken,
Nor ever be misunderstood.

Miracles Fall Like Drops of Rain

Communication plain as day,
Eternally unlimited;
Language with no words to say,
Completely uninhibited.
How far away from this are you,
Bound to the world you stay,
And yet, how near to it are you,
Just an instant's space away.

So look ahead but not behind,
To a world you do not want.
Cut the strings, unbind your mind,
All that glitters value not.
Esteem the things you seem to see,
And they seem real to your eyes—
Mere dust without reality
In a world meant to disguise.

Part I

You Must Decide Which World to View
(Inspired by ACIM Lesson 130)

You must decide which world to view,
For you can see but one, not two;
The world you see was made by fear,
And nothing seen is really here.

You cannot have some love and hate—
They're opposites that cannot mate.
True love can have no enemy,
But what you fear you cannot see.

The fear within has made you blind—
Mixed with guilt inside your mind;
Reality cannot be seen
When the choice is made for dreams.

The world you see is proof you made
The choice for fear, Love's barricade.
The world you see is quite consistent
From the point of view you see it.

Your projection makes perception—
A picture of the mind's reflection;
As you think you will perceive—
Change your mind for a reprieve.

You Cannot Fail to Find the Truth
(Inspired by ACIM Lesson 131)

You seek for goals that cannot be achieved
While lost in dreams that should not be believed.
You seek for safety on a battleground
And permanence that never will be found.
You seek the light where only darkness is
And stability in its antithesis.

Meaningless goals can never be attained
Through senseless means where nothing can be gained.
Pursuit of the imagined leads to death,
For while you seek for life, you ask for death.
You look for safety and security
And danger from a mind that is guilty.

Yet searching here is inevitable,
And you are free to choose another goal.
Beyond the place of every worldly thought,
There comes a thought reality has brought,
An old idea remembered but forgot,
Holding everything you really want.

You cannot seek in vain but can delay,
Deceive yourself in thinking hell's the way.
No one remains in hell for no one can
Abandon his Creator or His Plan.
All that you seek but this will fall away,
You will reach Heaven—it is here today.

Part I

There is no future, and there is no past;
The Will of God is now and can't be smashed.
For Heaven's still your one alternative
To this strange world you made in which you live.
God doesn't suffer conflict nor do you,
For His Creation can't be split in two.

How could it be God's Son could be in hell,
Yet be in Heaven by His Holy Will,
And give up truth but for a paradox,
Opposing thoughts meant only to flummox.
God did not make two minds but only one,
With Heaven the effect of being One.

There is a lighted doorway in your mind—
The door swings open with intent to find,
Illumination from a Light so clear
That every spot of darkness disappears.
Today God's ancient promise to His Son
Has healed his mind in the knowledge they are One.

Ideas Leave Not Their Source
(Inspired by ACIM Lesson 132)

What keeps the world in chains but you—
Insane beliefs you hold as true.
A madman thinks the world he sees
Is as real as can be.

Yet anyone is free to change—
The source of thoughts can be exchanged;
A hope of freedom comes at last—
It frees the future and the past.

In the present, the world is free
From fear and doubts and miseries,
For your beliefs have been released;
Thoughts of death have finally ceased.

The world is nothing in itself—
Your mind gives it meaning, nothing else.
What you see are your own wishes
Acted out and yet fictitious.

There's no world apart from what you wish;
God Himself does not punish.
Change your mind's wishes on what you see,
And the world must change accordingly.

We say *ideas leave not their source*—
The central theme of this, The Course.
There is no world! The central thought—
The Course attempts to bring about.

Part I

You are a *Thought* in God's own mind—
You still reside there, you will find,
And thoughts in yours that you projected
Are still there and can be rejected.

The sick are healed as you let go
Of thoughts of sickness that you know.
The dead arise when thoughts of life
Replace all thoughts of death and strife.

You are as God created you—
The world you see was never true.
Release the world and you will see—
Only your thoughts can set it free.

I loose the world from all I thought,
For I am real—the world is not.
I would know my own reality—
I remain as God created me.

Don't Value What Is Valueless
(Inspired by ACIM Lesson 133)

There is no satisfaction—
You've heard it said before—
In all the world's attractions
Seen outside your door.

The eminence you value,
Your bodily concerns,
To sorrow do they lead you
With imminent heartburn.

All the worldly things you see
The body does desire—
Are only temporary,
Leading to a funeral pyre.

They have no lasting value—
What fades was never there;
They offer nothing to you
And bring only despair.

If you choose to take a thing
Away from someone else,
It leaves you now with nothing
But denial of the Self.

And if you feel guilty
For the choices that you make,
Then the mind has served the body—
For sins are but mistakes.

Part I

For there are just two choices
The mind must recognize—
In one, spirit rejoices,
The other offers lies.

Don't value what is valueless—
Seek for what is true;
What's valuable is timeless,
And it belongs to you.

What Is True Forgiveness?
(Inspired by ACIM Lesson 134)

The world perceives forgiveness as a gift unjustified,
A sacrifice of righteous wrath where truth has been denied,
A pardon asked for what is true that smiles on a sin—
In such a view, this Course must rest salvation on a whim.

This twisted view of what forgiveness means must be corrected;
The fact that pardon isn't asked for what is true must be accepted.
It is irrelevant to everything except illusions,
And everything you seem to see are just the mind's delusions.

Because you think your sins are real, you see pardon as deception,
A treachery to truth where guilt is real in your perception,
And those forgiven from this view are mocked and twice condemned
By themselves for what they think they did and by those that pardon them.

It is sin's unreality that makes forgiveness sane,
A relief to those who offer it where sanity remains.
It does not allow illusions, but collects them without fear,
And lays them at the feet of truth to watch them disappear.

The ability to overlook what is not there opens the door
To truth, which has been blocked by dreams of guilt you held before.
When you feel that you are tempted to accuse someone of sin,
Ask instead, "Would I accuse myself of doing this?" and look within.

Part I

It's here you'll find the Voice for Truth and free your mind of guilt;
It is but lies that would condemn in your illusions you have built.
Forgiveness stands between the truth and dreams that separate
Between the hellish world of guilt and the path to Heaven's gate.

And now all dreams of death and hate are left outside the door—
No need to fight the dragons and the monsters anymore.
The armor made to chain the mind to fear and misery
Is tossed aside and left behind in a mind that's finally free.

Sickness Has One Attribute
(Inspired by ACIM Lesson 136)

Sickness has one attribute—
It's a defense against the truth;
It proves that what you made is real;
Reality it does conceal.

It sees what's whole in separate parts;
What was perfect falls apart,
Defenses made for self-deception,
Illusions that require perception.

The choice for sickness can be made;
A defensive strategy is laid.
When the truth knocks at your door,
It can threaten you no more.

You suffer pain within the body,
Proving that you must embody
The pile of dust you seem to be
That commands you die and cease to be.

The body triumphs all that's true
From its twisted point of view—
Stronger than the Will of God,
Atop its perilous façade.

And you believe that Heaven quails
Before such madness that prevails,
God made blind by your illusions,
The mind made in its own confusion.

Part I

But Heaven has not bowed to hell;
God hasn't changed His holy Will.
You can but choose to think you die,
But what you see is but a lie.

Your dreams you have made manifest,
Forgoing truth at your request.
Yet no illusions can remain,
When truth is asked to replace pain.

Sickness as the mind's defense
Hides the light and makes no sense;
You must give up insanity,
Allowing truth to set you free.

You Are Never Healed Alone
(Inspired by ACIM Lesson 137)

Sickness proves what once was One
Has now been torn apart,
And now it seems God's holy Son
Is separate from God's heart;
Held apart by sickened flesh
In a body that has crashed.

The world obeys the laws it made
That sickness seems to serve,
A guilty mind that is afraid
Where sickness seems deserved.
Its Self appears dismembered;
Unity is not remembered.

To be healed is merely to accept
There has never been a sin.
A simple truth you must respect
That stays forever as its been.
Healing then, must demonstrate
That God's own truth must be your fate.

Healing is a counter-dream,
Cancelling dreams of sickness;
Where illusions are what's seen,
It looks upon them with forgiveness.
Healing offers restitution;
It's the mind's own absolution.

Part I

As you let yourself be healed,
You heal those all around you.
The truth no longer is concealed—
Healing demonstrates it's true.
You are never healed alone;
The truth of Self is always One.

Heaven Must Be Chosen Consciously
(Inspired by ACIM Lesson 138)

In this dualistic world where choices must be made,
It seems there are alternatives to truth that are displayed.
All things have an opposite
In a world that contradicts,
For if a Heaven does exist, then there must be hell to pay.

In God's world of truth, creation knows no opposition,
But the truth can never enter in the world of fear's condition.
There is truth or there's illusion;
There is Oneness or seclusion;
And in the mind's confusion, conflicting goals are its position.

The obvious escape from opposites must be your choice;
Complexity will cloud your mind when you seek the ego's voice.
There is only one decision
In a world seen of division
That will end all your confliction and allow you to rejoice.

Now you may choose to use the world of time for transformation,
Different from its purpose now of hell's own demonstration—
Where hope changes to despair,
Of real life you're unaware,
Conflict is all that is now there, and death is your salvation.

Part I

Such mad beliefs can grip the mind with great intensity,
Defended against truth with fear and great anxiety.
It must be saved from its salvation,
While it fears its own damnation,
Without knowing its causation of its own insanity.

The only choice for Heaven must be chosen consciously;
Alternatives are clearly seen and looked at accurately.
All that's veiled in dark shadows,
From the minds own darkened gallows
Holds no terror now—it's brought into the light, and we can see.

Love Is Endless in His Oneness
(Inspired by ACIM Lesson 139)

The end of choice
Where I rejoice—
I hear One Voice
Above the noise.
There is no doubt
What I'm about—
I shout it out!
I shout it out!
I am free, I am free,
Just as He created me—
In perfect harmony,
In One reality.
There is no fear
Atonement's here
His Voice I hear
As Love appears.
Our happiness
Is all there is—
Love is endless
In His Oneness.

Part I

Bring Your Illusions to the Truth
(Inspired by ACIM Lesson 140)

The remedies the world accepts can never really cure;
The panacea they offer to the body does obscure.
It substitutes illusions for illusions in a dream,
But does not address the mind that engineered the crazy scheme.

The happy dreams the Holy Spirit brings are different—
The dreams forgiveness brings allow the mind to rest content.
His dreams are heralds of the dawn of truth upon the mind;
They lead from sleep to waking in the minds of all mankind.

Atonement heals with certainty and cures every form of sickness;
The mind lets go of idle dreams in favor of forgiveness.
There's no illness that can enter where all guilt has been released;
Atonement takes away the guilt and leaves the mind in peace.

Peace be to you who have been cured in God and not in dreams,
For cure must come from holiness where sin cannot be seen.
God is barred where sin has entered, yet there's no place where He is not;
Sin can have no place to hide but in illusions you have brought.

We lay aside our amulets, our charms and medicine;
We listen to the Voice of truth that releases every sin.
And to the remedy that truth provides we now can clearly yield,
As the mind that brings illusions to the truth has now been healed.

Let the Holy Spirit Be the Judge
(Inspired by ACIM Lesson 151)

You do not really question
What the body seems to see,
Though you've witnessed the deception
Of the senses frequently.
Your judgement rests on witnesses
That your senses offer you,
But the ego provides witnesses
That were never really true.

You've been cautioned against judgement
Not to withhold any rights,
But belief in ego's judgements
Is to lose your holy sight.
The ego guides your senses
To the guilt you have within;
It speaks to you of weakness
And reminds you of your sin.

But the truth of you is spirit,
Magnificent and pure,
But the ego will not hear it,
For its condemnation's sure.
You must learn to doubt its evidence,
To ever recognize your Self,
Behold not the body's senses
But hear the Voice for God Himself.

Part I

Let Him be the judge of you
And let Him judge your brother,
Because His Vision's always true
In the glory of the Father.
He is privy to the truth of you;
Your guilt He will erase
As He shares with you His holy view—
Of the rapture of Christ's face.

His lessons will enable you
To bridge the gap between
Illusions and what's really true
In everything that's seen.
He takes away the faith you have
In suffering and disaster,
And leads you to a world of love
And happiness ever after.

Suffering Is Your Decision
(Inspired by ACIM Lesson 152)

Suffering is your decision—
Sickness comes with your permission—
You give your own consent to die;
Guilt's your chosen alibi.
Nothing occurs but what you wish,
Choices that are outlandish.

God's gift of everything is yours—
Can this now be exchanged for wars?
Can pain ever be part of peace?
Joy abandoned for disease?
Can sickness enter in a mind
Where perfect holiness abides?

Salvation is the recognition—
Truth can have no opposition.
Nothing but the truth is true;
You are as God created you.
You must remain unchangeable,
Completely unassailable.

The world you see is what you made,
The sinful, guilty and afraid;
God knows not of the ephemeral—
The world He lives in is eternal.
This isn't God's reality—
It's a world made from insanity.

Part I

To think that God has made chaos,
And brought you here to suffer loss,
Where death triumphs over all life,
And everywhere is pain and strife,
Is arrogance upon your part,
When truth states *you can't be apart*.

It must then be your own decision,
To relinquish thoughts of sin.
To recognize God's Son implies
That self-concepts are laid aside.
No longer can they be believed—
Their arrogance has been perceived.

The radiance of God's own Son
Is now accepted as our own,
For this is true humility—
Accepting what God willed to be.
It's our right to Heaven as well,
And with it our release from hell.

Defenselessness Is Strength
(Inspired by ACIM Lesson 153)

A world seen of uncertainty in a rodeo's bullpen;
Gifts along the way are there and then they disappear again.
If you've felt threatened by this world of hurdles and setbacks,
The world provides no safety—it is rooted in attack.

Its "gifts" of seeming safety are illusory deceptions;
Peace of mind's not possible where danger threatens your perception.
Defensiveness is what is seen; threat brings anger righteously;
Everywhere is treachery, and there's no place for you to flee.

Escape no longer can be seen, and hope cannot be found;
Attack, defense, defense, attack— keeps the mind forever bound.
Defenses are the costliest of all the ego's fees,
Madness in a form so grim there's no hope of sanity.

You are its slave; you know not what you do in fear of it;
The holy peace of God is gone; your heart in iron grip.
You behold the Son of God as but a victim to attack,
In need of great defenses in his silly dreams of lack.

Defenselessness is strength— it recognizes Christ in you,
Its own weakness laid aside for the Holy Spirit's view.
It recognizes strength so great, attack is but delusion—
A silly game a child might play in a world seen of illusion.

Today, we look past dreams and see we don't need a defense;
We've left all fearful thoughts behind and come without pretense.
And in defenselessness we stand, sure of our salvation;
We choose the strength of Christ and hear the Voice of inspiration.

Part I

The Love of God Is All that's True
(Inspired by ACIM Lesson 154)

I listen to His heavenly Voice
It lifts me up above the noise
It whispers softly in my ear
There's nothing else I want to hear
It speaks to me of perfect love
The kind that I've been dreaming of
Embracing me in gentleness
With images that only bless
I'm peaceful now as I listen
He tells me that I'm without sin
The Love of God has always been
I simply need to look within
To find the Light that He put there
And learn to see it everywhere
Illuminated in my mind
Waiting there for me to find
I need to share it with the world
The Voice of Love, His holy Word
And so I say from me to you
The Love of God is all that's true
There isn't any other thing
Except the pain of suffering
But you can always let that go
If God is what you want to know
And if that is your only choice
Your One-True-Self will now rejoice.

Step Back in Faith and Let Him Lead the Way
(Inspired by ACIM Lesson 155)

There is a way of living in the world
That is not here, although it seems to be.
And those that walk as you do in the world,
They do not change but smile more frequently.

The world is an illusion that you made,
And those that come avoid reality,
But you can make the choice to let dreams fade
Behind the truth restoring sanity.

If truth demanded they give up the world,
It would appear that sacrifice was asked.
But there's another way within this world
To walk the path and let illusions pass.

The way to go is to accept the truth,
Allowing it to light the path ahead.
Illusions can no longer be the truth—
You hear the Voice for God within your head.

Your brothers have been given now to you
To follow in your footsteps as you go,
With certainty of purpose to what's true,
Away from death to happiness aglow.

Part I

Step back in faith and let Him lead the way;
The One Who Knows goes with you every mile.
We walk to God along this new pathway
That leads away from dreams of our exile.

He Lights My Mind with Happiness
(Inspired by ACIM Lesson 156)

I walk with God in perfect holiness;
There is no cause for guilt; it can't exist.
The Father can't be separate from His Son;
He shares Himself with me; the truth is One.

No attribute of His remains unshared,
As where He is, His holiness is there.
What shares His life is part of Holiness,
And lives within His perfect sinlessness.

There is a light in you which cannot die,
Whose presence now can only signify—
That dreams of death and punishment and sin
Have been let go and with a happy grin.

I walk with God in perfect holiness;
He lights my mind with only happiness.
The world I see before me I now bless;
I walk with God in perfect holiness.

Part I

Echoes of Eternity
(Inspired by ACIM Lesson 157)

In the silence of my mind
If I listen I can find
Echoes of Eternity
Crystal clear lucidity
Just a little glimpse of Heaven
Right beyond our own dimension
Shedding light on what I see

For a moment I am free

A different kind of feeling
I'm not seeing

    I am being

I am here
        and I am there

I am simply e v e r y w h e r e

There is nothing I am not
All my problems I forgot
I can see an open door
Where all learning is no more

For a moment there's transcendence

    Entering into
    His Presence

I'm unaware of anything
But the Perfect Love He brings

And I know this Holy Instant
But an instant's not sufficient
Yet at least I can remember

When there only was Forever

And my moment now is gone
But Your memory lingers on.

Part I

The Light We Shine Shines Back on Us
(Inspired by ACIM Lesson 158)

There is knowledge that was given you that never can be lost—
It was given to each living thing and does not have a cost.
The truth is that you are a *mind* and have never left your Source;
You are as He created you—He is your True-Life-Force.

The knowledge that the Father and the Son are One will come
In time to every mind, and yet in fact, that time is done.
The world of time and space is but a part of mind's delusion,
For time, just like the world you see, is just a vast illusion.

The journey that you make's already done, the script is written;
We review it in our minds while the ending still seems hidden.
The world the ego made was but corrected in an instant,
And yet time's grand illusion makes it seem a mighty distance.

You cannot give experience, but a teacher shares a vision—
There's a quiet place within the world where all has been forgiven.
All contradictions reconciled, it's here the journey ends;
Experience—untaught, unseen—is there and it transcends.

Our goal here is Christ's vision, and Christ's vision has one law,
For it does not see the body or its errors or its flaws.
It beholds a light beyond the body in God's perfect purity;
It sees this light in everyone, and all events it sees.

This can be taught and must be taught by all who would achieve it;
Nothing in the world compares with vision that perceives it.
See no one as a body; see the Son of God he is,
Acknowledging that he is One with you in holiness.

Miracles Fall Like Drops of Rain

Thus are all mistakes you see and everything forgiven—
In holiness, they disappear in the power of Christ's vision.
It matters not what form they took or how big they seemed to be;
They are no more, and all effects are gone eternally.

Your brother's not a body—he is spirit, as are you;
Your mind knows that his spirit is not separate from you.
How you see your brother is how your mind will see yourself—
If you see him full of sin, so you see yourself as well.

It matters not when revelation comes, from time its unaffected,
Yet time still has one gift to give where knowledge is reflected
In a Vision of His holiness so beautiful and pure,
That when its shared with all, it brings the love that will endure.

Today, we practice seeing, and we use His Holy Vision
As we look out past the bodies and see everything forgiven.
We shine this light on everyone and everything we see,
And the light we shine shines back on us in perfect Unity.

Part I

Christ's Vision Is the Miracle
(Inspired by ACIM Lesson 159)

The world believes "to have" means keep,
So different from Salvation,
That teaches what we give we reap—
There is no deprivation.

You understand that you are healed
When you offer only healing;
Heaven's fate is truly sealed
And found when you're forgiving.

Your brother is now recognized
As part of your true Self;
Forgiveness lifts the dark disguise—
It looks beyond itself.

Christ's vision is the miracle
That reflects Heaven here;
It conquers every obstacle
And eliminates all fear.

Every miracle is born
In Christ's holy vision,
In Spirit, mind has been re-born,
Ending all division.

Christ's vision is the holy ground
Where lilies of forgiveness,
Root and grow and can be found
To share beneficence.

Miracles Fall Like Drops of Rain

Take the treasures He provides,
As they're given, they increase;
Behold where miracles reside—
They lead to death's release.

Part I

Salvation Is Acceptance of your Self
(Inspired by ACIM Lesson 160)

You are a stranger to the ways of love,
And what you are is now unknown to you.
The truth of Self you cannot conceive of,
For fear exists in a state that isn't true.

There is a stranger in the Son of God,
And fear has taken residency here,
Ideas so foreign to the truth of God,
An alien possessed by his own fear.

Who is this stranger—is it fear or you?
Could you be made in the likeness of His fear?
If God is Perfect Love, then what are you?
The truth of Perfect Love casts out all fear.

There's nowhere that can shelter love and fear;
As opposites they cannot coexist.
If you are real, then fear cannot be here;
If fear is real, then you do not exist.

The truth is here; it cannot be concealed,
Who fears has but denied his One-True-Self,
And lives in exile on a battlefield,
His home denied, a stranger to himself.

And now it seems return's impossible—
A stranger to himself is not at home,
For what he needs now is a miracle,
But for God's Son a miracle will come.

For in God's home your One-True-Self remains;
No stranger has moved in to take your place.
It's only fear that keeps your mind in chains,
And fear can be exchanged for Christ's own face.

The Father's not a stranger to His Son,
And Christ is not a stranger to yourself.
What God creates remains forever One;
Salvation is acceptance of your Self.

Part I

Ask Your Brother for His Blessing
(Inspired by ACIM Lesson 161)

We take a stand against our anger that our fears may disappear,
And we welcome Christ into our minds and let His Love appear.
It's here Atonement's made complete and Heaven is restored—
In answer to temptation where fear and anger lived before.

What was the natural condition of the mind has gone awry—
Complete abstraction known before is no longer recognized.
It sees tiny fragments of the whole instead of all as One;
It invents the partial world you see; a dream world it has spun.

As every mind is One, and every mind contains all minds,
Every brother is all brothers, and this is the truth you'll find,
But the mind that thinks specifically can no longer grasp abstraction,
For mere words can bring no clarity nor lead to satisfaction.

Bodies are a symbol for a concrete form of fear,
Yet love does not need symbols— in its light, fear disappears.
But hate is more specific— it requires an enemy,
And the mind directs the body to attack the thing it sees.

The vision of the brother as a body does symbolize
The fear that we projected we don't want to recognize;
The unconscious fear and hatred we don't really want to see
Is projected onto someone else, and he's the enemy.

And now I must be innocent; my guilt is seen in you,
But the body is a symbol—it was never really true,
And the guilt that I projected on external enemies
Is still within my mind; the only enemy is me.

Miracles Fall Like Drops of Rain

To attack another body's simply to attack yourself;
The perception that I have of you I hold against myself.
If I see you as a body, hateful, wicked, full of sin,
The mind that's not apart from you will see this sin within.

To find the mind's release from sin, we use His holy Vision;
It looks beyond the body to perceive us both forgiven.
Your perception of your brother is the key to your salvation,
For love would not destroy itself but in imagination.

Ask your brother for his blessing and behold him in Christ's Vision—
Mind united in God's Spirit; there was never a division.
In the holy Light of God, he shines in perfect innocence,
And so you shine together in God's own magnificence.

Part I

I Am as God Created Me to Be
(Inspired by Lesson 162)

I am as God created me to be—
These sacred words I hold within my mind,
That lead away from darkness that I see;
Illusionary dreams are left behind.

There is no fear these words will not allay;
All thoughts of sin but fade before their might.
All dreams of death have forever gone away;
The mind is resurrected in His Light.

Our dreams are happy, and we rest secure;
The truth's illuminated in our minds.
Our safety certain, healing has occurred;
Our spirits are forever intertwined.

The Light has come to bless the world I see—
I am as God created me to be.

Death Is Gone, the Mind Is Finally Free
(Inspired by ACIM Lesson 163)

Death is gone; the mind is finally free—
There is no doubt and no anxiety.
Death as savior will not be worshipped here;
All gone is the embodiment of fear.

Deceptions held within its withered hands
Have been let go and with it the demands
Of punishment the guilty mind requires
With suffering and death as its desire.

We won't bow down to idols such as this;
What God creates as One with Him still is.
We will not worship death in any form;
To mind's illusions we will not conform.

There is no death for death is not Your Will;
Your Love shines on us, and our minds are still.
The life we share with You is all we see;
Our will is One with Yours eternally.

Part I

The Song of Heaven
(Inspired by ACIM Lesson 164)

An ancient melody so fine,
From far beyond the sounds of time;
Each note harbors a memory,
A long- forgotten symphony.

The song of Heaven faintly heard;
The Voice for God, His holy Word;
The Father's call you recognize—
You gloriously harmonize.

The Christ within that is your Self
Now answers echoing your Self.
He shares with you His holy Sight,
His Vision that is love's delight.

Together now you sing the song,
The harmony known all along,
From ancient peace within the heart,
That knows you've never been apart.

How easily are sins forgot;
Sorrows are remembered not,
Every single pain released,
And now exchanged for endless peace.

We stand forgiven in Christ's sight;
We bless the world in holy light.
The curtain has been opened wide,
Inviting you to step inside.

He Holds You One with All that Is
(Inspired by ACIM Lesson 165)

We are Thoughts within the mind of God,
We've learned— *ideas leave not their source.*
What could hide the truth that lies beyond
Withholding what's already yours—
But thoughts of death and misery
And denial of eternity?

The Thought of God created you;
From Him, you've never been apart.
You are as God created you;
He's your Source; you cannot be without.
He holds you One with all that is;
He is your Source of happiness.

Who would deny his Source of peace,
His joy and everlasting life,
And choose instead thoughts of disease,
Of pain, of suffering, and strife—
If he could only recognize
Where all his peace and joy abide?

Heaven's joy is there for you to find,
Just ask, and it is yours today.
Sight you can exchange for being blind,
Vision that won't lead you astray—
Where all denial is laid aside—
The choice to live where Love resides.

Part I

His Gifts Are Yours to Give
(Inspired by ACIM Lesson 166)

All things are given to God's Son; God gives without exception,
But if your will's not one with His, they are beyond reception.
This world that's seen is not God's Will, and so it is not true;
The mind that thinks it real is split; what's One now seen as two.

This fractured mind is fearful; it's forgotten what it is—
It believes it's a container in a world that seems amiss.
The magnificence of God Himself shrunk down into a body,
He seems an aging, frail figure lost upon a road that's rocky.

In poverty and loneliness, he wanders on while unaware,
That the gifts of God go with him and their treasure can't compare
With the valueless and temporary things in which you trust
That are here but for a moment before turning into dust.

He walks a road to nowhere through life's tragic corridor,
Never knowing God goes with him or of his treasures at His door.
He walks with pain and misery where the end is always death,
Never knowing when the ax will fall and steal his last breath.

This is the self you've chosen, the replacement that you made,
That you savagely defend against while truth has been mislaid.
Your head stuck down into the sand with blinders on your eyes,
In fear you scream and cower lest the truth you recognize.

The Voice for God calls to you, holy Son, look at your gifts;
Would you relinquish poverty, and pain and death for this—
The magnificence of God Himself—He shares Himself with you,
Immortality Divine and perfect Love that's always true?

It's not God you have imprisoned in your plan to lose your Self;
He knows not about your plan to turn you into something else.
There was a need He did not understand to which He gave an Answer,
And you who have this Answer now need nothing else but laughter.

The wish for death is answered, and your sight replaced with Vision
By the One who walks with you who knows there was never a division.
He reminds you that you dream a dream whose content is not true,
And if you're sad or fearful, He is always there with you.

He lights your mind, and now His touch has made you like Himself,
And the gifts He offers to you must be shared with your whole Self,
For the gifts of God He shares with you are not meant for you alone,
And it's only as you share them that you will know them as your own.

And now His gifts are yours to give, entrusted to your care,
To share with all your brothers now who walk still unaware
Of the Light that is within them that will shine away all fear
By releasing all the darkness as they let His Love appear.

Part I

When Dreams of Pain and Death Are Gone
(Inspired by ACIM Lesson 167)

In this world, there appears to be a state—
The opposite of life that God creates.
You call it death; it comes in many schemes,
All sorrow, loss, all pain and suffering.
They all acknowledge death as what is true,
Believing God can be split into two.

Death is the thought that you could separate
From your Creator and could demonstrate,
Success in proving ideas can leave their source,
While lost in dreams of bodies and remorse.
The mind can choose what it would like to see,
But what it sees is not reality.

The mind can think it sleeps and live a lie,
Believing it's a body that can die,
But it can never change its waking state
By dreaming dreams of death as its own fate.
What seems to die is the sign of mind asleep,
Attached to dreams the mind must want to keep.

When mind elects to be what it is not,
Existing in a state of opposites,
Assuming powers it does not possess,
A separated state of much distress,
And yet the truth can never be exchanged,
All Thoughts of God remain always unchanged.

The mind asleep is lost in dreams of time,
And time is but a foolish paradigm,
Where all that seems to be has not occurred;
A dream of pain and death has been preferred,
But when the mind awakes, it carries on;
All dreams of pain and death are finally gone.

There is One Life; we share it with our Source;
Reality has never gone off course.
God shares perfection with His holy Son,
With Heaven the effect of being One.
We are as He created us to be,
Forever One for all eternity.

Part I

Request His Grace and It Is Yours
(Inspired by ACIM Lesson 168)

If you understood the meaning
Of the Love God has for you,
You would quickly wake from dreaming
Now in favor of what's true.

Despair would be impossible
And all hope now satisfied,
For there can be no obstacles
When His Will is recognized.

Request His grace, and it is yours—
For your acknowledgement it waits.
Love's remembrance is in store,
And all gone are dreams of hate.

His grace restores all memories
The sleeping mind forgot,
While lost in endless reverie
Where real love is not.

In grace you see a Light that shines
and holds the world in Love's embrace.
It is salvation's final sign
Fear has gone and been replaced.

Grace
(Inspired by ACIM Lesson 169)

Beyond the world entirely,
Grace leads me to this destiny;
It cannot come until the mind
Has been prepared and now inclined
To have and hold it willingly.

Within the world of hate and fear,
Grace is the state of Love held dear.
Acceptance of the Love of God,
It sees beyond the world's façade,
And only truth does it revere.

Grace is not learned; we must prepare,
Allowing mind to come aware
Of things it does not know to date,
Being ready to accept a state
Completely different from what's there.

Grace foreshadows Heavenly Light
And sees the world with holy Sight.
Experience that grace provides
Comes to an end where time resides
In pure Illumination bright.

Part I

We ask for grace in which to live;
We offer grace, and this we give.
For grace releases everyone;
It sees the holy truth of One.
Our only goal is to forgive.

There is No Cruelty in God
(Inspired by ACIM Lesson 170)

No one attacks a brother without hurt as an intention;
To attack in self-defense is to be cruel as protection.
You believe to hurt another brings the freedom you revere
And leads to something safer that alleviates your fear.

Attacking to defend from fear is thoroughly insane,
For here fear is protected, fed, and endlessly maintained.
You make what you defend against, defending makes it real;
It's only when you lay your armor down that truth's revealed.

This enemy that you attack now seems to be outside you,
But by your own defense sets up an enemy within you.
A thought so alien to truth, depriving you of peace,
Your mind split now into two camps without hope of a release.

It seems love has an "enemy," and that enemy is fear,
And fear must now have your defense lest the truth of you appear.
For fear becomes your safety and protector of your peace,
And love's endowed with attributes of fear that just increase.

Fear's the obstacle to God that throws the mind off course,
The mind that thinks it's separate and divided from Love's Source.
When Love becomes an enemy, then cruelty is god—
Fear, attack, and punishment are something you applaud.

But the truth of you is Love itself; you have not left your Source,
There is no cruelty in God, and all His Love is yours.
Allow the block to be removed, return your mind to Him,
And fear is gone forever, and the world's no longer grim.

Part I

Now the peace of God is ours for we are just like You;
No cruelty abides in us for there is none in You.
We choose again and bless the world and everything we see;
In gratitude we find our peace; our minds are finally free.

The Truth of One Identity
(Inspired by ACIM Lesson 181)

When you attack a brother, you will find
Awareness of the truth has left your mind.
Your brother's limited by what you see,
But what you see is not reality.
The sin you see in him has left you blind.

But change the point of what you want to see
And what you see will change accordingly.
Relinquish focus on your brother's sins,
Restoring peace that comes from light within,
That holds the truth of One Identity.

If there's no sin in you, there's none in me;
There is no separation that I see.
We look past sin and seek for innocence
To make apparent only sinlessness—
The truth of Spirit and of Unity.

Part I

The Child in You
(Inspired by ACIM Lesson 182)

The world you seem to live in is not a home to you,
And somewhere deep within your mind, you know that this is true.
A memory keeps haunting you from a long-forgotten place,
And you feel like an alien here, exiled from outer space.

Some suffer in the games they play to occupy their time,
To keep their sadness from them and render life sublime.
He who walks the world in darkness for what he cannot find,
A thousand homes he builds but none will ease his restless mind.

He does not understand that what he builds, he builds in vain;
There's no substitute for Heaven; all you find here is but pain.
Is Heaven in your childhood home and reflections of your youth?
An old, distorted memory that never was the truth.

And yet there is a Child in you who seeks his Father's home,
Who knows he is an alien here with nowhere left to roam.
This Child gently calls to you with an innocence so pure—
He reflects the Love of Heaven and brings the Light that will endure.

You have not lost your innocence—it is for this you yearn;
This is your heart's desire, and to this Voice your head will turn.
This holy Child remains in you; his home is yours today;
Throw down your toys of battle now and let him lead the way.

I Call on God
(Inspired from ACIM Lesson 183)

God, God, God, God, come into my mind;
God, God, God, God, let your name I hear remind.
I call to You as Yahweh, and to Jehovah too;
Oh Mighty Lord I seek you; Adonai I call to You.

God, God, God, God, repeat the name and find—
God, God, God, God, relief to my split mind.
Holiness be to Allah, to Elohim I sing;
Hallelujah Jah, in Brahman is everything!

I Am the Alpha and Omega, before Abraham I Am;
All Glorious and Omniscient One, I Am Who I Am.
Oh Almighty Father, I am your cherished Son,
I am as You created me, and so we are as One.

It's this Your Name reminds me of, and on Your Name I call—
To awaken distant memories of time before the fall,
Before dreams of separation, of which I seek release,
Restoring mind to knowledge of Your own eternal peace.

Part I

Creation Has One Name
(Inspired by ACIM Lesson 184)

You make a name for everything,
Each symbol a separate entity;
Space is laid between all things,
Carved out of perfect Unity.

A world of illusions you have made—
Think not that it is true;
Perception is the price you paid
To hold a separate view.

There is a name to call your Self
From where your spirit dwells;
Can you really separate yourself
From something else?

Use all your names and symbols
From the world that darkness rules,
But symbols can't be sinful
If they share God's name with you.

God's name is our salvation,
And escape from what we made;
His name unites the nation
Lost in the masquerade.

The Peace of God
(Inspired by ACIM Lesson 185)

You say you want the peace of God, but do you really mean it?
Many people say these words, but very few have meant it.
No one can truly mean these words and simply not be healed;
You cannot play with dreams without believing they are real.

You are the hero of your dream and to each the dream is different,
The outcome wanted not the same to each hero's intent.
Loser and gainer shift about in ever changing patterns—
Today you win at his expense, next time you're lost and tattered.

To say you want the peace of God means giving up illusions—
You've looked at them and realized they're simply mind's delusions.
Another dream would offer nothing more than all the others;
They all bring pain and misery to you and to your brothers.

No one who truly seeks the peace of God can fail to find it;
The peace of God is yours, and for you peace was created.
No one can lose, and all must gain when God's gifts have been received;
The hope that lies beyond despair in His peace can be perceived.

Part I

It Depends on Me
(Inspired by ACIM Lesson 186)

Your Father still remembers you,
And of this, I am certain;
You have a role assigned to you,
Dim the lights and raise the curtain.

There are two roles that you can play—
They lead to different places;
One has a hefty price to pay,
One leads to love's embraces.

All false humility is laid aside,
So we may hear His Voice—
His function for us He will provide,
Your spirit will rejoice.

There is one way, and only one,
To release you from your prison—
Let the ego be undone,
And the Christ in you has risen.

The Grace of God Is in Everyone
(Inspired by ACIM Lesson 187)

I bless the world, and it is me I bless,
And all I give is what I must possess.
The world thinks now that what I gave is lost,
But what is *real* can never have a cost.

Extend ideas and you will finally find
That those ideas are strengthened in your mind.
The peace you share with all belongs to you,
And when you bless, the Father blesses you.

Illusions that you see must disappear;
The Holy Spirit's Voice of Love you'll hear.
You must release ideas of suffering
And sacrifice that dreams of darkness bring.

For there can be no place for sacrifice—
Its presence proves that you have closed your eyes,
And now, correction for it must be made,
The gift of lilies on the altar laid.

At last, the altar to One God is sought,
And Spirit's welcomed—we are One in thought.
Fear's forever gone in Love's eclipse;
His Love's extended from our fingertips.

The world we see is one we now would bless;
His Sons shine brightly in His holiness.
The grace of God is seen in everyone,
And every single thing we look upon.

Part I

The Light You Seek Is Still Within
(Inspired by ACIM Lesson 188)

Those who seek the light are only covering their eyes,
You need not wait for Heaven, but you still must recognize
The light you seek is still within; this light you seek is yours;
You brought it from your native home from Him Who is your Source.

This light can never become lost; you can't deny its presence;
It is not hard to look within and find its luminescence.
God's peace is shining in you now and from your heart extends
A blessing to each living thing forever without end.

The shining in your mind reminds the world what it forgot,
And restores His memory to you in the dreams that you begot.
Salvation is now yours to give, and it radiates from you,
The Light of God that blesses everyone you give it to.

The Love and holy peace of God can never be contained—
When it's extended from yourself, a piece of it remains
Within yourself, it multiplies exponentially,
And now it's seen in everything, universally.

Thus our minds have been restored, releasing us from strife;
The peace of God still shines in us and all that share our life.
For we've absolved the world from everything we thought it did—
Our vision is restored at last from the light the darkness hid.

Blinded by the Light
(Inspired by ACIM Lesson 189)

There is a light within you
That the world cannot perceive,
For the world you see has blinded you
From the light that you've received.

It was not placed within you
To be kept hidden from your sight,
For you must see the world anew,
Innocent and shining bright.

The world you see is now transformed—
It rejoices that you came.
It keeps you safe from every form
Of danger and of pain.

It offers you a gentle place
In which to stay a while;
It blesses you with God's own grace—
Its love will make you smile.

This is the world His Love reveals,
So different from what you see;
The darkened world that fear conceals
Is not reality.

This world reflects the quietness
And peace that shines in them,
The innocence and gentleness
From wells of joy within.

Part I

And now what would you choose to see?
The choice is given you—
A world of love and true mercy
If you feel God's Love in you.

If hatred finds a place in you,
The world you now will fear,
But choose the Holy Spirit's view,
And a world of love appears.

I Choose the Joy of God
(Inspired by ACIM Lesson 190)

Pain is proof of self-deception—
It is not a fact at all.
Testament to your misperception,
You cannot hear the call.

Pain proclaims that God is cruel,
A sign illusions reign;
Insanity becomes the rule,
God's Love exchanged for pain.

Peace to all this foolishness,
The time has come to laugh!
Let all your nightmares be addressed—
Don't write your epitaph!

It is your thoughts that cause you pain;
There is no cause but you;
The dismal sound of life's refrain
Need not be listened to.

The world you see does nothing;
It can never be the cause—
A dark and dreary smokescreen
For the ego's guilty laws.

Nothing external to your mind
Can injure you at all;
It's all projected from your mind—
For pain, your wishes call.

Part I

Lay down the sword of judgement
That you hold against *your* throat;
Let God's joy be triumphant—
Deception's antidote.

I Am the Holy Son
(Inspired by ACIM Lesson 191)

I am the holy Son of God—
Declare it to the world;
Deny your own identity,
And madness is unfurled.

Despair will snatch every scrap of hope
As you assail the world alone,
Dangling at the end of rope,
With love being unknown.

What is it but a game you play,
Where Identity is denied?
You are as God created you—
Mind must be rectified.

I cannot suffer pain, I'm told,
I cannot suffer loss,
Nor fail to do what salvation holds—
Let Spirit be the boss.

A miracle will light your way,
All dark and ancient caverns
Where rights of death linger in your mind—
We'll break those ugly patterns.

All power is given unto you
In earth and into Heaven;
There is nothing that you cannot do,
When God is your intention.

Part I

Let the Son awake from his charade
And open up his eyes;
Return to bless the world he made,
And lift the dark disguise.

I Have a Function
(Inspired by ACIM Lesson 192)

It is your Father's holy Will
That you complete Himself,
This is the function you must fill
So you can be your Self.

Forgiveness is your function here—
Untruth must be undone;
There is nothing in the world to fear
If we are truly One.

Creation is not of the world—
It has no meaning here;
The knitted dreams that you have purled
Will unravel—just don't fear.

The Holy Spirit takes your pain;
He transforms all your dreams—
The joyful sights that they contain
Will release you from your screams.

So hold no one a prisoner—
Release and you're made free;
The way is simple to be sure—
The Son deserves mercy.

You hold the sword above your head—
Avert or fall, you now must choose;
If you condemn, you end up dead—
Your neck is in the noose.

Part I

He is as God created him,
And you are what he is;
See now that you are One with him
And forgive him all his sins.

All Things Are Forgiveness Lessons
(Inspired by ACIM Lesson 193)

God Wills the Son eternal happiness—
With peace and joy, he is forever free;
Forever gaining scope and limitless,
He's still as God created him to be.

And yet the Son believes he's something else—
He needs but a correction for his sight.
The Light of Heaven shines on all his ills
To make perception beautiful and bright.

The world you see before you is not real,
And all must be forgiven in your sight;
The truth the mind would like you to conceal
Must be pulled out and looked at in the light.

You are the cause of all your suffering;
Forgiveness is the only cure there is.
The Son can't be a guilty, frail thing;
He must be seen in total sinlessness.

Now each event that comes along your way
Gives you another chance to see the light.
The lessons seen on any given day
Require adjustment from His holy Sight.

The truth is obvious and very clear—
Forgive, and you will see this differently,
Allowing every sin to disappear—
The world of darkness changes instantly.

Part I

When you are tempted to think pain is real,
And death becomes your choice instead of life,
Remember it's forgiveness that will heal,
Releasing you from bondage and of strife.

These are the words that rid the mind of fear,
Allowing sin to go and hurt no more;
I will forgive, and this will disappear—
You hold the key that opens Heaven's door.

Place the Future in His Hands
(Inspired by ACIM Lesson 194)

We place the future in the Hands of God;
The goal of Heaven is in sight.
The path now sure with the certainty of God;
The future is absolutely bright.

How close we are to approaching our true goal,
Releasing every single sin.
Separation's now exchanged for being Whole;
We hear the Voice for God within.

God holds your future, and you now should know
Your past and present for sure too,
For they are always one to Him, and so
They should be one to you now too.

Yet in this world the temporal progression
Still seems real, that is so.
You need not understand time's retrogression—
You must just let the future go.

The past is gone away now, and at last
It is freed from your perception.
Suffering's forever in the past,
The holy instant in conception.

Now place your future in the Hands of God
And peace is reflected in your mind.
His memory will fill your mind with love,
Temptation forever left behind.

Part I

Walk in Gratitude the Way of Love
(Inspired by ACIM Lesson 195)

Your brother's not your enemy,
Because he's not a friend to thee;
He's in your mind; you misperceive—
The Oneness you do not believe.

You are separate from no living thing;
Give thanks, your mind is opening.
An ancient door is swinging free,
Releasing all your brothers and thee.

Let gratitude become the rule—
When you compare, you are a fool.
Give thanks but in sincerity,
Aware now of the Unity.

Walk in gratitude the way of love,
Freeing the mind to soar above
The battleground you see below;
God loves you more than you can know.

Gratitude will pave the way
And shorten your distance day by day,
For love can walk no road alone;
God gives you thanks—you are His own.

I Crucify Myself
(Inspired by ACIM Lesson 196)

When this is firmly understood and kept in full awareness,
You will not attempt to harm yourself or be a slave to vengeance.
You will be free
Of insanity
When all attack is seen,
With your own head in the guillotine.

Thus do you teach your mind that you are not an ego,
And liberate yourself from thoughts that only lead to sorrow.
Liberation does unwind
The resurrection of the mind,
Leading us from bondage
To the state of grace that God Is.

The dreary, hopeless thought that you can make attack on others,
And escape yourself, has nailed *you* to the cross and not your brothers.
Perhaps it seemed to be salvation—
You didn't see the devastation,
A belief in fear
You still hold dear
Of angry gods bent on damnation.

Part I

Such is the madness you believe; you must accept it too—
The fear of God is real to all who think this thought is true.
Foolishness is not perceived;
Insanity must be believed;
A shift in your mind
Would be most kind,
And the thoughts that bring you fear will be relieved.

When the fear of God is gone, no obstacles remain
Between you and the peace of God—there cannot be a pain.
The enemy that is seen without must now be seen within.
Step back from your fear
And love will appear—
Release ideas of sin.

It's My Gratitude
(Inspired by ACIM Lesson 197)

You make attempts at kindness
And then turn them to attack;
You don't realize your blindness
When you must get something back.

With gratitude or lavish thanks
Your gifts must be received,
Or love's withdrawn with inner angst,
And not to be believed.

And so you think God's gifts are loans,
Deceptions that would cheat you.
Ensuring when He strikes your bones,
He will not fail to beat you.

You know not what your thoughts can do,
Weakness now salvation,
So claim your strength or you will rue
Your lack of liberation.

The world thanks you when you release
It from all your dark illusions.
The gifts you give you will receive
When you give up all your delusions.

Your gratitude is all your gifts require
Offered from a thankful heart,
And love is what you will acquire
From God's most grateful heart.

Part I

God blesses every gift you give;
They're given all to Him,
And every time that you forgive,
Heaven sings a hymn.

My Forgiveness Sets Me Free
(Inspired by ACIM Lesson 198)

True injury is impossible,
But condemn, and you'll be hurt.
Illusion seems unstoppable—
Laws of truth do you subvert.

Condemn and you're a prisoner,
Forgive, and you're made free.
What *seems to be* did not occur—
Forgiveness is your key.

Forgiveness is the only road
That leads out of disaster,
Past all the suffering you behold—
It leads to Heaven after.

You hold the answers in your hand—
Now thank the One who gives them;
His words you may not understand
At first, but you can learn them.

His words will work, his words will save—
They come with Heaven's Love;
His words are born of God and pave
The way to up above.

My condemnation injures me;
My own forgiveness sets me free;
The truth bestows these words on thee,
That in them you might find the key.

Part I

Repeat them one more time for me—
The end of darkness it will be.
My condemnation injures me;
My own forgiveness sets me free.

I Am Free
(Inspired by ACIM Lesson 199)

Freedom is impossible;
The body is an obstacle;
The mind can only become free
When the body is no longer seen.

The ego holds the body dear,
Firmly tied and full of fear.
The ego then is quite insane,
Shackled, hateful, full of pain.

Beyond the laws of time and space,
To the Holy Spirit the mind must race;
Unlimited it then will be,
Forever strong and always free.

Attack thoughts cannot enter here,
What rests in God will never fear.
The body is a useful form
When given to Spirit to transform.

A vehicle which can extend
Forgiveness to all without end;
This is your all-inclusive goal
That you must reach with heart and soul.

I'm not a body, I am free;
I hear the Voice God's given me—
It's only this my mind obeys;
We stand as One released today.

Part I

The Peace of God
(Inspired by ACIM Lesson 200)

Save yourself the agony of bitter disappointments,
Bleak despair and hopelessness, and misery's appointments.
You can't make peace of chaos, nor is there joy in pain;
You will not win through losing—there is nothing there to gain.

Ask for love and happiness, eternal life in peace,
Gifts already given you, and they can never cease.
You do not have to seek for hell to see where Heaven lies—
It's through the door that welcomes you—just open up your eyes.

This world is not where you belong; you are a stranger here;
You search the world for meaning, but there is no meaning there.
You will be bound till all the world is seen by you as blessed,
And everyone made free of *your* mistakes and so addressed.

Peace is the bridge that all will cross to leave this world behind,
And when it's recognized at last, it heals your shattered mind.
There is no peace that you will find, except the peace of God,
And when you realize this truth at last, you will applaud.

INTERMISSION

Intermission

Forever One, Forevermore
(A Spiritual Ode to E.A. Poe)

Once upon a dream so weary, after lifetimes I did query,
Why salvation was not found in all the things I did adore,
As my mind began unwrapping all the ego's darkened trappings,
I perceived a gentle tapping at my mind's internal door—
And a quiet Voice did whisper that I never heard before—
    It's only Me, you're looking for.

As I pondered on the whisper, while my ego did but whimper,
Did my mind pick up a fissure that had not been there before?
While I feared my mind was cracking in the silence now
   nerve-wracking,
Was the "something" I was lacking not a thing outside my door?
The emptiness I felt inside with pain one can't ignore—
    Had that unlocked an ancient door?

The Voice of Spirit growing stronger, in my mind, ignored no longer,
Voice of God or voice of serpent, I ask now, who do You work for?
And the Voice so soft and gentle, it could never be judgmental,
Spoke of God so fundamental that my mind could not ignore—
Could this Voice for God I hear *be* what my mind was searching for?
    There was a knocking on the door.

So, I asked the Holy Spirit— since I no longer seemed to fear It—
How do I rid myself of suffering that seems to be forevermore?
The pain I have is frightening, and my mind is not enlightening,
And the fear I have is heightening as I get closer to death's door—
And the Holy Spirit answered me as He answered me before—
    It's only Me you're looking for.

His gentle Voice assured me and after time, it reassured me,
And the love of God secured me in awareness never known before,
But the ego started fearing as His Spirit was appearing,
For the mind was finally clearing from the thoughts it held before—
Thoughts of sacrifice and suffering born from separation's core—
    In the ego's dreams of war.

And the ego, now uncertain, feared the lifting of the curtain,
While it held each tiny hurt in, while the blame must be offshored,
And the guilt that it provided, in the dreams that were misguided,
Could be easily subsided if the Voice was not ignored—
The gentle Voice of Spirit that the angels do adore—
    There was a creaking of the door.

Now the Holy Spirit taught me that God had not forgot me,
It was He, that had begot me—He was still my Guarantor,
And the Son that He created, as a Whole and consecrated,
This could not be separated, except in dreams of nevermore—
The ego's dreams of darkness that the mind chose to explore—
    That shut the mind's internal door.

Intermission

For the truth of me was spirit, and this spirit had God in it,
And with me, my brothers shared it, just as they had in days of yore,
While the world that seemed so real, was just a smokescreen to conceal
The guilt the ego seemed to feel from the madness that it bore—
From the "tiny mad idea" that spawned the world that it asked for—
    Heaven was seen no more.

But only God's reality—can be the truth—I guarantee—
And all you see that seems to be are only dreams that you explore.
What God created One is One, you still remain your Father's Son,
And when the ego's dreams are done, the separation is restored—
The salvation of the mind is done, the Son will sleep no more—
    A beam of Light shone through the door.

The Holy Spirit spoke to me of God's undying love for me,
In Him, I share Identity, and it's only Him my heart yearns for,
But the truth I need to recognize as dreams of death have closed my eyes—
I've listened to the ego's lies and shut the mind's internal door—
Asleep in dreams of darkness in the ego's art of war—
    It's time to open up the door.

How can this be accomplished, can the ego be abolished?
With the body as accomplice, how can the mind now be restored?
The Voice for God assured me, just as the ego once had lured me—
It was God that did secure me in the Oneness I longed for—
The Oneness that still exists behind the mind's internal door—
    Just what I was looking for.

Miracles Fall Like Drops of Rain

It is the grievances you hold against your brothers you uphold
That keeps the mind in a blindfold without the light that you long
   for;
The mind supports allegiances to all your petty grievances,
And now it thinks that's all there is in this world you now deplore—
This darkened world of pain and death the ego does adore—
    That keeps you stuck outside the door.

Not until all is forgiven through the Holy Spirit's Vision
Will the end of the division be seen again once more,
For each error that you tally in the ego's vengeful rally,
Keeps your lilies in the valley and your altar way offshore—
The lilies of forgiveness that *your* mind is asking for—
    That will open up the door.

For spirit can't be broken and each grievance— thought or spoken,
Is the ego's ugly token that it's still your mind's mentor.
For the spirit seems divided as the mind has been misguided,
Each sin held against another is but held against your
   Self—forevermore—
For there's nobody else out there but *your* spirit you abhor—
    Forever One, forevermore.

But God sees all forgiven, in these dreams you *seem* to live in,
There was never any sin in dreams of guilt the ego bore,
For your dream of separation is not shared in God's Creation,
So the mind's Illumination is what you should be looking for—
The gift of God's own grace that blesses all forevermore—
    Forgiveness opens up the door.

Intermission

And now my mind's delighted for it no longer is blind-sighted,
And His Vision now has lighted up my mind like Heaven's shore!
For a moment in eternity could not break the continuity
Of the Father's perfect Unity with the Son that He adores—
His only One Creation that still is One forevermore—
    The ego—is nevermore.

PART II

Part II

Forgiveness
(Inspired by ACIM Workbook Part II, #1)

Forgiveness does not pardon sins—
To do that makes them real;
It simply sees there was no sin—
The truth it does reveal.

What is sin but separation?
God seems separate from his Son;
This was not God's legislation,
For His truth is always One.

An unforgiving thought is
A judgment that condemns;
Distortion is its purpose,
Guilt projected onto them.

In frenzy it pursues it goals,
Twisting what it sees;
Unforgiveness is the role
To smash reality.

Forgiveness as the Course is taught,
In stillness it does nothing;
It looks, and waits and judges not—
God's truth is what it brings.

I Wait and Listen for Your Voice
(Inspired by ACIM Lesson 221)

Father I come to You today
To seek Your Love to guide my way;
In the quiet of my heart I wait
To hear Your Voice communicate.

Let all my random thoughts be still
So I can hear and know Your Will;
In silence I will hear Your call,
Your Voice that speaks of Love for all.

We wait with only one intent—
To hear the Voice that's Heaven-sent,
No longer doubting we are One,
As You reveal Yourself to Your Son.

God Is My Source
(Inspired by ACIM Lesson 222)

God is my Source
The One life force
The air I breathe
The ground beneath.
The Spirit which directs
My actions to reflect
The Love that I choose
The water which renews.
He is my home
The star of my poem
He gives me His Thoughts
So I'm not distraught.
He covers me with kindness
Removing the blindness
From all that I see
When He shines on me.
Your Name on my lips—
A total eclipse
Of my mind in Your Presence,
The peace of Your Essence.
And now I ask to
Rest in You
In peace a while
To make me smile.

I Have No Life but God's
(Inspired by ACIM Lesson 223)

I was merely mistaken—
I thought we lived apart,
Separate and forsaken,
From God's unloving heart.

And now I see my error,
I'm the dreamer of the dream;
I no longer live in terror
Of a god that makes me scream.

Now I know my life is God's,
I have no other home;
We never really were at odds
On these lonely roads I roam.

I don't exist apart from Him—
He's not apart from me;
I have no thoughts that aren't of Him;
Through Christ I choose to see.

To home we would return today,
We're lonely here alone;
It seems so long we've been away
From where we are at home.

Part II

God Is My Father
(Inspired by ACIM Lesson 224)

I don't know where I'm going,
Nor what it is I do;
Perception's replaced knowing—
Idols replaced You.

I've forgotten my Identity,
Still, it's known to You.
I'm weary of the world I see,
I've lost my gift from You.

And yet my true Identity
Is glorious and great;
The gift my Father gave to me
The ego can't negate.

Only this is my reality,
The Love that God extends—
The gift of perfect Unity,
It's here illusions end.

God's Love Is Blazing in My Mind
(Inspired by ACIM Lesson 225)

You've given all Your Love to me
For now and through eternity;
Love radiates its kindly Light
And illuminates my new-found sight.

I know that when I give it back,
It stays with me without a lack;
When the love flows out of me,
The channel opens joyously.

The way back home is finally found
And real happiness abounds.
Your Love is blazing in my mind—
Forever more we are entwined.

Part II

My Father Awaits My Glad Return
(Inspired by ACIM Lesson 226)

A dream of separation was all it ever was,
An answer to a mad idea, insanity the cause.
It's your mind that gives it value, sparkles in your eyes,
Illusions and false idols, an enchanting dark disguise.

But if I see no value in the world as I behold it,
And have not replaced reality with illusions to uphold it,
What need have I to linger in a place of vain desires—
A world of shattered dreams and the pain that guilt requires?

My real home awaits me and my gratified return,
Replacing dreams of madness with the love for which I yearn.
My Father's arms are open and with mine they intertwine;
I don't have to wait for Heaven for it's already mine.

My Will Is Yours
(Inspired by ACIM Lesson 227)

It is today that I am free, because my will is Yours;
I thought to make another will disconnected from my Source.

Yet nothing that I thought apart from You exists for me;
The illusions that I made did not affect reality.

Now I give them up and lay them down for Him to find,
Allowing them to be removed forever from my mind.

The Son of God lays down his dreams and leaves them in the past,
Released from sin with his right mind restored to him at last.

Part II

My Father Knows My Holiness
(Inspired by ACIM Lesson 228)

My Father knows from where I came;
His holiness I share—
Accept the truth as He proclaims—
And I haven't got a care.

I was mistaken in myself,
I failed to realize
The Source that is my One-True-Self
And open up my eyes.

My mistakes are only dreams—
I let them go today,
And hear the Voice that has the means
To lead me not astray.

I take His word for what I am—
He knows who is His Son.
A part of Him is what I am,
And so, we are as One.

Love I Must Be
(Inspired by ACIM Lesson 229)

Love I must be, the truth of me,
If God is what created me.
I need not seek a moment more;
I stand before an open door
And claim my true Identity.

The only truth that there can be,
My Father kept it safe for me;
I cannot question anymore—
Love I must be.

His Love is what created me,
The holy face of Christ of see.
Serenity has been restored;
Insanity is nevermore.
We stand in perfect Unity—
Love I must be.

Part II

I Seek His Peace
(Inspired by ACIM Lesson 230)

In peace I was created;
In peace do I remain;
I was never separated—
God's peace is my domain.

How merciful the Father is,
His peace forever true;
Peace *is* what the Father is—
It's always shared with you.

I am as God created me—
I have the gifts He gave;
Peace is God's reality—
His peace can only save.

Salvation
(Inspired by ACIM Workbook Part II, #2)

Salvation is God's promise that you would find your way
Out of all the hell you made when your mind went astray.
It guarantees that time will end, thoughts born in time will cease,
Every thought of conflict will be replaced with thoughts of peace.

The Thought of Peace was given you the instant your mind split;
There was no need of such Thoughts before, peace had no opposite.
The Thought that has the power to heal became part of every mind
That failed to see that it was One—the truth it now could find.

Salvation is undoing; it fails to support
The world of dreams and malice that perception would report.
Salvation, then, does nothing, but it lets illusions go,
Without support they fall away, and into dust they blow.
And what they hid is now revealed— an altar to His Name—
With gifts of your forgiveness laid, His memory you'll claim.

Come daily to this holy place and spend a while within—
It's here we share our final dream, given us by Him.
In this dream there is no sorrow; it holds his Holy Sight,
Night is gone forever; we come together in the light.

From here we give salvation, for it's here it was received;
The sound of our rejoicing is the song we will perceive.
The Father is remembered, and all our dreams are done;
Unity is not dismembered; Heaven's joy remains as One.

Part II

Father, I Seek You
(Inspired by ACIM Lesson 231)

Sometimes I seek for something
That will fill the void in me,
The empty, endless hunting,
For a magic remedy.

Yet what but Your Love heals?
Who but You can ease the pain?
Why listen to the ego's appeals
When empty dreams are what remain?

Father, I seek but You today—
There's nothing else I want to find;
Spirit help me find my way—
Let Your Love heal my mind.

A Prayer to God
(Inspired by ACIM Lesson 232)

Be in my mind
When I awake,
That I might find
Your Love to take
To shine on me
Throughout the day
And always be
The only way.
Let every minute
Be a time
With You in it
So sublime,
And let me
Not forget
Our hourly
Minuet.
Please be there
To hear my call
Whenever
I might slip and fall.
As evening sets
My thoughts are still,
I can't forget
Your Love fulfills.
In You I sleep

Part II

My safety sure,
Your peace I keep
Your Love is pure.
Certain of Your care
To You I run,
Happily aware
I am Your Son.

Be My Guide
(Inspired by ACIM Lesson 233)

I give You all my thoughts today
That You might help me guide my way;
I give You all my acts as well,
That when I act, I do Your Will.

I seek the path that You've ordained,
Not seeking goals I can't obtain.
I will step back and follow You,
Who gives me wisdom that is true.

Whose tenderness is without end,
And Love I cannot comprehend,
Which is the perfect gift for me,
For now and in eternity.

Part II

When Dreams of Sin and Guilt Are Gone
(Inspired by ACIM Lesson 234)

Today we can anticipate
The time when we can celebrate,
When dreams of sin and guilt are gone,
And the holy peace of God is won.

An instant in eternity
Couldn't break the continuity
Of thoughts forever shared as One
Between the Father and His Son.

Your memory we cannot lose;
Your perfect Love we can't refuse.
We accept the truth of this today;
In gratitude to You we pray.

Your Holiness Is Mine
(Inspired by ACIM Lesson 235)

I need but look upon all things that hurt or cause me fear,
And with the certainty of God, watch them disappear.

His Will for me is happiness, no other will than this,
Then happiness must come to me if my will is joined with His.

God's Love surrounds His holy Son and keeps him always sinless,
Safe forever in His Arms without need of forgiveness.

The Father's holiness is mine; it is forever true.
I have no guilt or sin in me, for there is none in You.

Part II

I Rule My Mind
(Inspired by ACIM Lesson 236)

The kingdom of my mind is mine—
This kingdom I must rule;
Sometimes it seems to get off line—
A misdirected tool.

It seems to triumph over me,
And tells me what to do,
What to think and who to be—
It's not worth listening to.

And yet the mind can only serve—
The purpose I must choose;
The ego I must not preserve,
Or joy is what I lose.

Today my mind will serve God's Will,
No other thoughts but this.
My mind the Holy Spirit fills;
My will is One with His.

I Am as God Created Me
(Inspired by ACIM Lesson 237)

Today I see
The truth of me,
My destiny
In God's glory.
The light in me
Will shine on thee
And guarantee
God's reality.
This, my Father's call to me
To share in His Identity—
No blasphemy
Can there be
In our perfect Unity.

Part II

His Light Shines in Us
(Inspired by ACIM Lesson 239)

We will not hide in false humility
The truth we share of Our Identity.
We will be thankful for the gifts He gives;
We see His Glory in all that we forgive.
He Loves His Son forever without end;
The Love He shares with us we now extend.

Forever loved in perfect constancy,
Without a trace of guilt or sin to see,
We thank the Father for the Light that shines
Upon All He created as Divine.
We honor it—His Light we can't eschew;
United in this Light were One with You.

Fear Is but Deception
(Inspired by ACIM Lesson 240)

Fear is but deception; you can't be the things you see—
A mental misconception of impossibility.
It does not matter what the form appears to be—
Be not deceived,
Let the truth be received;
We are a part of Love itself— this must now be believed.

The world you see but witnesses to all your dark illusions
Of yourself and of the world, the mind's scary delusions.
The focus on what is not true will leave your mind in ruins.
Let go of your fear;
Throw down your spear;
Recognize the Son of God, and let His Love appear.

Part II

The World
(Inspired by ACIM Workbook Part II, #3)

The world's a false perception, born of error and mis-thought;
It remains while it is cherished in the pain that guilt has wrought.
It was meant to be a place where God Himself could enter not,
Perception born, and knowledge lost, a separation thought.

When the thought of separation has finally been released,
Replaced with true forgiveness and the mind returned to peace,
The world now seen in God's own Light, there is nothing now to fear;
The world we made will vanish and its errors disappear.

Your sight was made to lead away from truth as you uphold it;
Follow now His Light and see the world as *He* beholds it.
Hear His Voice alone in all that speaks to you each day,
And He will give back all the peace you thought you threw away.

Let us not rest until the world is joined in One perception,
Forgiveness made complete without erroneous deception.
To save the world we must then see it through the eyes of Christ,
That what was made to die is given everlasting life.

The Holy Instant of Salvation
(Inspired by ACIM Lesson 241)

It's a day of graduation,
A time of special celebration,
The mind's darkened desecration
Released to glorious salvation.

There is hope across the nation,
No more quiet desperation,
A united population
In a forgiveness demonstration.

And at last the desolation
Of the mind's deterioration
Is returned to restoration
In God's own Illumination.

Part II

I Will Not Lead My Life Alone
(Inspired by ACIM Lesson 242)

I will not lead my life alone today—
I do not know what's best.
I give the reins to One who knows the way
And put my mind at rest.

I won't delay my coming home at all—
I make no choice myself.
To follow Him is to become it all,
One with my true Self.

And so, Father, we give this day to You—
We come with open minds.
Yes, the Holy Spirit always knew
Your Love is what we'd find.

Today I Give Up Judgements
(Inspired by ACIM Lesson 243)

It is impossible to comprehend
A vision of the whole from little parts.
I'm certain that the tail I see's the end;
You're certain that the trunk's the only part.

There is an elephant that's in the room—
Perception's left us blind; we cannot see.
The truth is missing, but we still assume
That we can judge our own insanity.

Today I give up judgements I can't make,
Allowing all creation to be free;
I honor all its parts and won't forsake
A single part of My Identity.

Your memory remains in every Son;
Your truth must shine in all of us as One.

Part II

Your Son Is Safe
(Inspired by ACIM Lesson 244)

Your holy Son is always safe, wherever he may be,
For You are always there with him for all eternity.

He need but call upon Your Name, and he will quickly find
Safety from the things he sees, and peace will fill his mind.

How can fear or doubt prevail, when he belongs to You?
Forever loved, forever blessed, God's Love is always true.

No storms can threaten our true home; His Light we cannot dim,
For what can threaten God Himself? Give thanks— we're part of Him.

Father, Your Peace Surrounds Me
(Inspired by ACIM Lesson 245)

Father, Your peace surrounds me,
No matter where I go.
It sheds its light on all I meet,
To lift those feeling low.

I bring it to the desolate,
The lonely and afraid,
The suffering and desperate,
Bereft of hope and aid.

Send them to me, Father,
Let me bring Your peace with me,
For I would save my brother—
In him, Your face I see.

And so we give Your peace today,
Your message we've received;
The Voice for God shows us the way—
Your Love will be believed.

Part II

I Choose to Love Your Son
(Inspired by ACIM Lesson 246)

To God you will not find your way
With hatred in your heart today,
And if you try to hurt God's son,
The peace of God is now undone.

The Father now you cannot know,
Awareness of the Self must go.
Your mind no longer can conceive
The love Your Father has for thee.

I will accept the way You choose,
The way for me to come to You,
And in that way, I will succeed,
Releasing hatred that impedes.

I recognize that what You Will
Is mine as well— I will fulfill.
Our destiny with You is One,
And so I choose to love Your Son.

Forgiveness Is the Only Means
(Inspired by ACIM Lesson 247)

If I behold sin in my brother,
I will be the one to suffer;
Forgiveness is the only means
Where my vision becomes clean.

If I accept what His sight shows me,
I'm the one who is healed completely.
Brother let me look at you—
Your sinlessness reflects mine too.

We stand forgiven, you and I,
The Holy Spirit cannot lie.
His Vision is the Light we see—
It holds our perfect Unity.

The Son of God Is One
(Inspired by ACIM Lesson 248)

I have disowned the truth about myself;
I have forgotten my Identity.
What grieves can't be a part of my true Self;
Whatever fears can't be part of me.

All pain is but illusion in my mind;
What dies was never in reality.
Beliefs I once held true, but now I find
Did hide the truth of my Identity.

Father, my ancient love for you returns,
And I accept the truth of Your Own Son.
We've been released from insanity's sojourn,
And now we know the Son of God is One.

Forgiveness Ends Our Suffering
(Inspired by ACIM Lesson 249)

Forgiveness ends all suffering;
It lifts the clouds that madness brings;
Loss becomes impossible
And joy becomes unstoppable.

Attack has gone without defense;
Anger makes no common sense.
The world becomes a joyful place;
Sin is gone without a trace.

So like Heaven are the effects,
The Light of God that it reflects;
The journey of the fall of man
Ends in the Light where it began.

We now return our minds to You—
We choose the Holy Spirit's view;
Gone are thoughts of fear and loss;
We are as You created us.

Part II

Behold the Son of God

(Inspired by ACIM Lesson 250)

Brother let me look at you,
But in the Holy Spirit's view.
Your glory now is what I see—
Gone is all your frailty.

You are God's very holy Son;
Illusions now have come undone.
Gentleness is seen instead,
And to the Father we are led.

Sin

(Inspired by ACIM Workbook Part II, #4.)

Sin is but insanity; the mind's been driven mad,
And seeks to let illusions take the place of what it had.
It dreams it is a body separated from its Source
In a race that leads to nowhere on an endless obstacle course.

The body is the instrument the mind made to deceive;
A device of separation, without knowledge, it perceives.
Disconnected from its Source, and mad, it now believes in lack;
A madman's dreams are frightening, and the fearful must attack.

And yet what sin perceives is but a silly, childish game;
The Son of God's a body prey to evil, guilt and blame.
Loss of all vitality, diseased, and short of breath,
Eternity exchanged for a brief life that ends in death.

How long, oh Son of God, will you maintain this game of sin—
Playing in a war against yourself you cannot win?
And all the while, you've never been without your Father's Love—
Its's time to wake and now give up the sin that you dream of.

Part II

A Song for God
(Inspired by ACIM Lesson 251)

I sought for many things, and I only found despair;
I searched for satisfaction and found it nowhere.
My searching was all in vain—
All I ever found was pain;
My life without you was a nightmare.

But now I see the Light—my eyes are opening;
My dreams are gone; in Him I need nothing.
The peace of God is finally in me,
And His Love, it sees right through me.
He's restored my mind, and I have everything.

God's Son Is My Identity
(Inspired by ACIM Lesson 252)

God's Son is my Identity—
Its truth is perfect purity,
A brighter light than any star,
You've looked upon from very far.

Its love is always limitless,
Because from God it's given us.
It burns with an intensity,
Yet calm in quiet certainty.

Beyond this world is my true Self,
The boundless Love of God Himself.
Its magnitude I can't conceive;
Its holiness I must believe.

God knows my true Identity—
He has revealed it now to me;
There is no other truth I see—
Heaven is restored to me.

Part II

I Rule My Destiny
(Inspired by ACIM Lesson 253)

The world is what I made it;
God did not create it.
His world is always perfect;
My world is my mind's effect.

It is my mind's projection,
An unholy reflection.
My mind is the director,
As well as every actor.

It's I who rule my destiny,
And what I see I want to be.
The truth I have forgotten;
In God I am begotten.

Illusions I must then let go,
If the Self I want to know.
He's the Father; I'm the Son—
And yet the truth is we are One.

My Mind Is Finally Still
(Inspired by ACIM Lesson 254)

In silence I would come to You to hear Your holy Voice;
I have no other prayer than this— to hear You and rejoice.

Your truth is what I want to know; Your truth is but Your Will.
Your Will I wish to share with You; Your truth I will fulfill.

When ego thoughts invade my mind, I pause and let them go;
I do not want what they would bring; It's You I want to know.

My thoughts now hallowed by Your Love; my mind is finally still;
I've chosen to remember You and know Our holy Will.

Part II

God's Peace is Mine
(Inspired by ACIM Lesson 255)

It does not seem that I can choose to have God's peace today,
But if I choose to hear His Voice, it won't lead me astray.

If God is Love and God is peace and I am just like Him,
The Love of God must be in me—His peace must be within.

Let me this day have faith in Him Who says I am God's Son,
And witness to the truth of what He says—His peace is won.

The peace of God was given me; it is forever true;
The Son of God can have no cares; there's nothing he must do.

I give today to finding what my Father Wills for me;
His peace I know as mine when I have shared it now with thee.

And so I share God's peace with you, and this is what I find—
The peace of God is still within, forever in my mind.

God Is My Goal
(Inspired by ACIM Lesson 256)

When sin is cherished in the mind,
The way to God is hard to find;
The road seems long and very far
To find the way to where you are.

It's easy to remain asleep,
In clouds of doubt the mind would keep;
Here we can but only dream,
Of God that still remains unseen.

In this world we seem to live,
The way to wake is to forgive;
Forgiveness is the only way
To hear His holy Voice today.

And when God is your only goal,
Forgiveness pays the guilty toll
Of a mind that still believes in sin,
To hear the Voice that is within.

Part II

No One Serves Opposing Goals
(Inspired by ACIM Lesson 257)

It is with determination,
That the mind can find salvation.
It's easy to become confused—
Unsure of who I am, I lose.

No one serves opposing goals,
And remembers well his One-True-Role.
The mind that's split cannot function
Without distress and dysfunction.

Forgiveness is the chosen means
To wake us from the world of dreams;
Our purpose must be Yours as well,
The breaking of the ego's spell.

Our Goal Is God
(Inspired by ACIM Lesson 258)

Remember that our goal is God—
We must then train our minds;
The ego's goal is to maraud—
Attack is what it finds.

God's memory we hide away,
Pursuing pointless goals,
Which only lead the mind astray,
Acting out the ego's roles.

Our goal is but to follow
In the way that leads to You;
In despair we will not wallow—
It's the truth we will pursue.

We have no other goal than this—
Your Vision we will see,
And when our will aligns with His—
He's our Identity.

Part II

Sin Is the Thought
(Inspired by ACIM Lesson 259)

Sin is the thought
That guilt has brought
That makes God seem
Outside the dream.
Sin blinds us
To the obvious;
God as a goal
Is unattainable.
It's *our* back
That sin attacks,
The source of fear
The mind holds dear.
And what but sin
Blocks the light within—
Separation
Is not salvation.
It but obscures
The Light that's pure
And what remains
Is quite insane.
The source of fear
That now appears
Where love is sought
In its opposite.
And now I see

The insanity—
The choice of fear
That I hold dear;
God is the Source
The One-Life-Force
Of all that is—
His Love it is.

Part II

Let Me Remember You Created Me
(Inspired by ACIM Lesson 260)

I did not make myself—I thought I did—
But I remain exactly as I was.
The light within, the darkness only hid—
I'm still but an Effect but not a Cause.

I have not left my Source, I never could,
And what I see are illusions in my mind.
Remember my Identity—I would—
And my own sinlessness is what I'd find.

I wish to waken from an endless sleep;
Let me remember You created me,
And from illusions to the truth I leap—
Your memory returns, and I am free.

We are your Sons; we come to You at last—
The time of separation's finally past.

The Body
(Inspired by ACIM Workbook Part II, #5)

The body is a fence around a Glorious Idea,
A device of separation, a splintered mind's panacea.
It is within this fence it lives, keeping Love away,
While all the while the body does but crumble and decay.

The Son of God's impermanence is "proof" his fences work,
And do the task the mind assigns where insanity does lurk.
For if His Oneness still remained untouched, who could attack?
Who could win and who could lose? In Oneness there's no lack.

The body is a dream you made, and just like night-time dreams—
It sometimes pictures happiness, but fear invades the dream.
Fear is where all dreams are born, and they always end up here,
But Love only creates the truth, and truth can never fear.

The body is the fence you made to keep yourself in hell,
Yet choose the goal of Heaven, and His Love will now dispel
All your dreams of darkness that the ego wants to keep,
Exchanging them for sanity—His happiness you'll reap.

One with God or one with flesh, the choice is yours to make.
You will identify with what you think will make you safe.
Identify with Love, and you are home; there is no fear;
Identify with Love, and your true Self is what appears.

Part II

In Him Is Everlasting Peace
(Inspired by ACIM Lesson 261)

In God is my Identity,
My refuge and security,
The only Source of strength in me,
The Light in which I choose to see.

Within Him is the only place
Where dreams of sin cannot erase
The memory of who I am—
And what He is, is what I am.

In Him is everlasting peace;
His Love for me will never cease.
For idols, then, I will not seek;
I choose to hear His Spirit speak.

I would come home to You today,
And let Your Spirit lead the way.
I am as He created me,
And only this I want to be.

You Have One Son
(Inspired by ACIM Lesson 262)

The Father has but just One Son; he is your One Creation,
And he, I choose to look upon without my condemnation.
For I am but a part of him; he is a part of me;
The brother that I seem to see shares my Identity.

A thousand names I've given him when only one will do;
A thousand forms I seem to see from my distorted view.
And yet Your Son must bear Your Name for You created him;
He's not a stranger to me for we really are akin.

Today we would but recognize the truth about ourselves—
Your peace and Love are shared with us and there is nothing else.
You share your One-True-Self with us in Love eternally,
United in Your Love we rest, in perfect Unity.

Part II

God's Spirit Is in All Things
(Inspired by ACIM Lesson 263)

God's mind created all that is—
His Spirit entered into it;
In purity and loveliness,
His perfect Love gave life to it.

Can dreams of madness be my choice,
Refusing then to hear His Voice,
A witness to belief in sin,
When what He is, is still within?

While we remain outside the gate,
Heaven still remains our fate.
We must see through His holy Vision
And not perceive any division.

Let all we see seem pure to us,
Within each thing God's innocence.
We walk to Him, His holy Sons,
United in His truth as One.

Salvation's Prayer
(Inspired by ACIM Lesson 264)

Father, Your Love surrounds me;
You stand before me and beside me;
You are in every sound I hear,
When I'm with You, time disappears.

You're in all things I look upon;
Only Your Love protects Your Son.
There is no other Source than this,
We all share in Your Holiness.

There's nothing but Your One Creation,
Within Your Love that holds the nation.
Your Son's exactly like Yourself,
Made from Love, he's Love itself.

We come to You in Your Own Name,
To share Your peace our only aim.
We join with You in this today;
Salvation's prayer is what we say.

Part II

I Laid My Sins Upon the World
(Inspired by ACIM Lesson 265)

I laid my sins upon the world and saw them looking back at me;
What I feared was in the world was not what it appeared to be.
I was deceived;
I misperceived;
What seemed to be was in my mind and not to be believed.

The world I see is shining bright in glorious Luminescence!
I see no sin, and nothing hides the reflection of His Holiness.
There is no fear;
Love has appeared;
My mind is One with His at last—the light I see is clear.

Do Not Forget His Name Is Yours
(Inspired by ACIM Lesson 266)

Father, You gave me all Your Sons;
Your Self was shared with everyone.
They're my saviors and counselors in sight,
The bearers of Your holy Light.

Do not forget from where they came!
Do not forget Your holy Name!
Do not forget his holy Source!
Do not forget his name is Yours!

This day we enter Paradise—
We finally open up our eyes,
Acknowledging the Self in all—
United we have heard the call.

Part II

In His Peace I Do Rejoice
(Inspired by ACIM Lesson 267)

Surrounding me is all the life created in God's Love;
It calls to me in every breath no matter where I rove.
In every action, in all thoughts, I'll go to any length,
Every heartbeat brings me peace; each breath gives me His strength.

Now it seems my mind is healed—His Vision I can see,
And all I need to save the world is given now to me.
I am a messenger of God, directed by His Voice,
Sustained by Him in Love, in His peace I do rejoice.

We Are Safe in His Identity
(Inspired by ACIM Lesson 268)

I will not distort creation—
I will simply let it be,
And accept His revelation
Of our One Identity.

In His Love I was created—
In His Love I will remain;
It's not that complicated—
Only truth is free of pain.

What is there that can frighten me?
There cannot be a loss;
We are safe in His Identity—
Let Spirit be the Boss.

Part II

The Holy Face of Christ I See
(Inspired by ACIM Lesson 269)

Father bless my sight today,
And show me my mistakes;
Your Holy Spirit guides my way,
No matter what it takes.

His Vision shows the truth to me—
I see a world forgiven;
The holy face of Christ I see
Through the Guide You've given.

Today our sight is blessed indeed—
We share one holy vision;
His gentle lessons will succeed—
The Son of God has risen.

Christ's Vision Is His Gift to Me
(Inspired by ACIM Lesson 270)

Christ's vision is Your gift to me—
It translates what the body sees
And shows me a forgiven world,
A glorious and gracious world!
How much more I will perceive
With His Sight that I receive.

The world forgiven signifies
The son has opened up his eyes.
His dreams are finally released;
His mind is finally at peace.
God's memory returned to him;
His vision is no longer dim.

His function now is but Your Own,
And every thought but You is gone.
The quiet of today will bless
Our hearts with Heaven's happiness.
His peace will come to everyone—
The Son will know itself as One.

Part II

Christ
(Inspired by ACIM Workbook Part II, #6.)

What is Christ but God's own Son as He created Him?
He is the Self that we all share, the Self that knows no sin.
He is the Thought which still abides within the mind of God;
He has not left His holy home, despite the mind's facade.

Christ's the link that keeps you One with God and guarantees
That separation was nothing but the mind's insanity.
Christ is the holy part of you in which God's answer lies;
It remains untouched by anything perceived by body's eyes.

Christ remains at peace within the Heaven of your mind,
The only part of you that has reality you'll find.
For within Him the Father placed the means for your salvation,
When dreams of death are given Him, exchanged for revelation.

The Holy Spirit reaches from the Christ inside of you—
To translate all your dreams into the truth is what He'll do.
When forgiveness rests upon the world, separation is erased;
Peace has come, and nothing blocks the vision of Christ's face.

Let us seek to find Christ's face and look on nothing else,
The Christ whom God created as His Son is our true Self.
The goal of the Atonement then has now been reached at last—
The vision of Christ's face is seen; the days of time have passed.

Christ's Vision Is the Way to You
(Inspired by ACIM Lesson 271)

Today I choose to look upon what Christ would have me see—
The Witness to the truth He brings of my Identity.

In Christ's sight, the world of sin is gone and with it fear;
The memory of God returns—perception disappears.

I listen to God's Voice and seek the truth in God's creation,
And see a world redeemed from death in joyous celebration.

Christ's vision is the way to You—the mind is sanctified,
The Father and the Son are One, creation Unified.

Part II

Can Illusions Bring Me Happiness?
(Inspired by ACIM Lesson 272)

Heaven is my one true home—
This truth belongs to me,
And all the roads I seem to roam
Are not reality.

Can illusions bring me happiness?
Can silly dreams content me?
Father, I will accept no less
Than *all* that You have given me.

Only Your Love can satisfy—
I'm forever safe in You.
Today, we pass illusions by,
Accepting what is true.

And if temptation calls to me
To linger in the dream,
I choose my true Identity,
And let His Love redeem.

His Peace Is What I Choose
(Inspired by ACIM Lesson 273)

Undisturbed tranquility
Is easily achieved,
For this is God's own gift to me—
It's there to be received.

The stillness of God's peace is mine
And nothing can intrude—
On the stillness of my mind
I've received with gratitude.

What need have I to fear
That I could somehow lose
The peace You give that I hold dear—
Your peace is what I choose.

Part II

The Voice of Love Is All We Hear
(Inspired by ACIM Lesson 274)

I seek the truth and let the Light replace
The veil of darkness hiding Christ's own face,
And so, today, I let all things just be,
As You created them for me to see.

Now with this truth, I'm finally redeemed
From all the darkened visions I have dreamed.
As truth has entered where illusions were,
The Holy Spirit's Vision is the cure.

My brother now is seen without a sin;
I see in him the Light of God within.
The Voice of Love, the only thing we hear,
And gone forever every form of fear.

Your Healing Voice Protects
(Inspired by ACIM Lesson 275)

Today I hear the Voice for God which speaks an ancient lesson,
I seek to hear and understand, releasing my suppression.
The Voice for God tells us of things we can't understand alone;
We cannot learn apart from Him—His Love for us is known.

Your healing Voice protects, and so I leave all things to You;
I need not have anxiety as You'll tell me what to do,
Where to go, to whom to speak and always what to say,
What thoughts to think and give the world—Your Voice shows me the way.

Part II

Have You Heard?
(Inspired by ACIM Lesson 276)

Have you heard
His holy Word?
God's Son is pure
And will endure.
In God created
And celebrated,
He shares with me
His Identity.
We must accept
And not reject
His Fatherhood
And our brotherhood.
We can't deny
The Self of "I"
It's right on par
With who we are.
We will not dim
The Light of Him
Who gave His Word
That we all heard.
His Word is mine
And it defines
My One-True-Self
That is myself.

The Son of God Cannot Be Bound
(Inspired by ACIM Lesson 277)

The Son remains but unassailable,
Not bound by law; he is forever free.
He is not changed by what is changeable;
He's still as you created him to be.

Unhappiness, he's undeserving of;
Defenseless, he needs no security.
He knows no laws except the law of Love,
Remaining in a state of purity.

We will not worship idols anymore;
We make the choice to end our slavery.
We see the Light beyond an open door;
We are the Father's Son forever free.

Part II

Dreams of Fear Have Left My Mind
(Inspired by ACIM Lesson 278)

If I'm imprisoned by a body,
My Father is imprisoned with me,
And I must believe in a world of lies,
Where all that seems to live must die.

I am lost to all reality,
And bound to all my frailties.
The Father now, I cannot know;
The truth of Self I do forgo.

Father, I ask for truth today,
That all my fears You would allay,
Instead of madness I would find,
That dreams of fear have left my mind.

Our Freedom Is Already Won
(Inspired by ACIM Lesson 279)

The Son of God has closed his eyes—
He's long forgotten paradise;
He dreams a dream that he's not free,
And believes it is reality.
He waits in chains for his release,
And does not know he has God's peace.

In reality, his dreams are gone—
His freedom is already won.
The chains that bind have all been cut;
The ladder out is standing up.
So why does he remain in chains,
Lost in dreams of fear and pain?

Today's the day I will accept—
Your gift of freedom I collect.
All my faith is given You;
I choose the Holy Spirit's view.
The Father forever loves His Son,
And now to You, I choose to run.

Part II

I Give Honor to the Son of God
(Inspired by ACIM Lesson 280)

I am a Thought within the mind of God, a complete extension of Himself.
No Thought of God has left the Father's mind, no Thought is limited at all.
No Thought of God is but forever pure, each Thought a part of God's true Self.
Can I lay limits on the Son of God, when His Father willed he have it all?

Today I give honor to the Son of God, for thus I find my way to You.
I lay no limits on the Son You Love, the Son you created limitless.
The honor that I give to him is Yours, and so it's shared with me now too.
What is Yours belongs to me as well—it's shared in perfect holiness.

The Holy Spirit
(Inspired by ACIM Workbook Part II, #7)

The Holy Spirit mediates between illusions and what's true;
His perception leads to knowledge from the grace that God imbued.
His truth is shared with everyone who chooses His clear sight;
Your fearful dreams he takes from you and dispels them in His Light,
And there all sights and sounds have been forever laid aside,
The witnesses of fear exchanged to those of Love we have denied.

When this goal has been accomplished and learning has achieved
The only goal it has in truth, God's Love will be believed.
The Holy Spirit guides you to the outcome He perceives,
And gives the means to go beyond—Eternal Truth you will receive.

If you but knew how much your Father yearns to have you see
The beauty of your sinlessness in God's reality,
You would not let His Holy Voice appeal to you in vain,
While clinging to the dreams you made of fear that still remain.

From the realm of Knowledge, the Holy Spirit calls to you,
To let forgiveness rest upon the dreams that you would view.
Restoring sanity at last and with it, endless peace;
The dreams you made to terrify yourself have finally ceased.
The Holy Spirit is the Father's gift He gave to you,
To lead you home to Him at last in Heaven's rendezvous.

Part II

I Must Confess
(Inspired by ACIM Lesson 281)

When I am hurt in any way,
Who I am has been forgotten,
And when my thoughts lead me astray,
My separate thoughts I'm caught in.

I've put meaningless ideas in place
Of where Your Thoughts belong,
And now I cannot see Christ's face;
I cannot hear Your song.

The Thoughts I think with You can bless;
Those Thoughts alone are true;
My separate thoughts make me confess
That I've forgotten You.

Your Name Is Love and So Is Mine
(Inspired by ACIM Lesson 282)

I will not be afraid of love today—
I will not be insane;
Asleep in dreams of death I will not stay,
While the truth of love remains.

I choose to recognize the Self today,
Whom God created "Son."
The Holy Son He loves I won't betray;
Our Identity is One.

Father, Your Name is Love and so is mine;
We cannot change what's true.
Fear's name is a mistake that can't define
The Self we share with You.

Part II

No False Images
(Inspired by ACIM Lesson 283)

I made an image of myself, and this I call God's Son,
Yet Your creation's as it always was for it is still as One.

Let me not worship idols today—I am the Son God loves;
My holiness is Heaven's Light—its Source is God's own Love.

Is not what is beloved of the Father still secure?
Is not the Light of Heaven infinite and still as pure?

I'm still as You created me—creation has not changed,
We share in His Identity—fear for Love has been exchanged.

Thoughts that Hurt Can Be Rejected
(Inspired by ACIM Lesson 284)

I can change all thoughts that hurt;
The pain I feel I can avert.
When rightly perceived, loss is not loss—
There is no grief at all with *cause*.
Suffering is but a dream,
But God's own truth must still be seen.

This is the truth that must be said
To get this idea inside your head.
It must be repeated many times—
Partial acceptance may take a long time.
Partly held with reservations,
Then with serious considerations,
Finally, the truth can be accepted—
Thoughts that hurt can be rejected!

I go beyond these words today,
Past reservations that I'd allay,
Arriving at a full acceptance,
Of the truth of full remembrance.
What God has given cannot hurt me,
So grief and pain there cannot be.
Let me not fail to trust in You,
Accepting only Your joy as true.

Part II

My Holiness Is Yours
(Inspired by ACIM Lesson 285)

Today I wake with God's own joy;
Forgiveness is my only ploy.
I ask for only joyous things,
Releasing all my suffering.

My holiness I do accept;
Grief and loss I do reject.
For what's the use of pain to me,
If I give up insanity?

Father, my holiness is Yours,
Because you are my only Source,
And now I can rejoice in You—
Forgiveness has restored my view.

There's a Kind of Hush
(Inspired by ACIM Lesson 286)

The hush of Heaven holds my heart;
No longer can we be apart.
This is the day that has been chosen
As the time to learn the lesson—
There's nothing that I need to do;
All choices have been made in You.

In You all conflict is resolved,
And every problem has been solved.
In You is all I hoped to find—
Your peace and Love are finally mine.
My heart is quiet; my mind's at rest;
Your Love is Heaven— I will attest.

In the stillness of today,
We hope that we have found the way;
We've traveled far to reach our goal—
In taking up our One-True-Role.
We trust in Him and in our Self,
The Oneness promised by God Himself.

Part II

You Are My Only Goal
(Inspired by ACIM Lesson 287)

Where else but Heaven could I go
If my happiness I want to know?
What gift is there I could applaud
Before the holy peace of God?
What treasure could I seek and keep
Next to the gifts of God I'd reap?
And would I rather live in fear
Than choose to let God's Love appear?

Father, You are my only goal—
You share with me Your only Soul.
What but You could I desire,
From whose Love I will not tire.
And what except Your memory
Results in my serenity?
It is but You that gives the means
To signify the end of dreams.

My Brother Is My Savior
(Inspired by ACIM Lesson 288)

There is a secret you must know that leads you to the Father—
You cannot make your way to Him unless you bring your brother.
You must first recognize what God created One with you,
And look past his own container to the spirit that is true.

I ask for help forgetting all my brother's past today—
This is the thought that leads to You without a long delay.
Now his sins are in the past, and with them so are mine,
And I am saved—the past is gone; our joy is genuine.

Let me not attack the savior you have given me to find,
But honor him who bears Your Name remembering it's mine.
My brother is my savior—let me overlook his sin,
And behold the Light of holiness that comes from God within.

Part II

Let Me Not See a Past that Isn't There
(Inspired by ACIM Lesson 289)

Unless the past is over in my mind,
I cannot see the truth—my eyes are blind.
The sights I see were never really there,
And all I see is darkness everywhere.

For my perception of the world is skewed,
From here the real world cannot be viewed.
The past is there to hide it from my sight;
The truth can only be seen in the light.

Let me not see a past that isn't there,
That's full of guilt and leads me to despair.
If there's no past, then there can be no sin,
For what else but the past is forgiven?

Your Own replacement for the world I made,
That's free of all the guilt that I have laid,
Untouched by sin, is there for me to find,
When dreams of guilt and sin have left my mind.

My Happiness Is What I See
(Inspired by ACIM Lesson 290)

Unless I look on what's not there,
My happiness I see;
The Love of God is everywhere—
Christ's vision comes to me.

What I perceive without correction
Is frightening, it's true;
I will not let my mind's deception
Believe in dreams untrue.

My happiness I seek today;
Your Love is what fulfills.
I seek Your strength to lead the way
And seek to do Your Will.

You cannot fail to hear me
Or give me what I ask for;
My happiness is what I see—
Love opens up the door.

Part II

The Real World
(Inspired by ACIM Workbook Part II, # 8)

The real world's a symbol, the opposite of what you made;
It can't be seen with eyes of fear where terror has been laid.
The real world can't be perceived except through eyes that bless,
Where witnesses to sin are gone and forgiveness is professed.

The real world holds a counterpart for each unhappy thought
Reflected in the world you see insanity has brought.
It corrects the sights of terror and the fear your world contains,
Replacing them with happy sights and releasing all your pains.

What need has such a mind for thoughts of murder and attack,
When safety, love and joy could be perceived instead of lack?
The world it sees arises from a mind that is at peace—
Because it's kind, no danger lurks in anything it sees.

The real world's the sign that dreams of sin and guilt are done;
The Son of God no longer sleeps; his joy has just begun.
The reflection of the Father's Love has been perceived at last;
The real world but signifies the end of time has passed.

Now God can take His final step and time has disappeared,
Leaving truth to be itself, God's memory now appears.
We look on a forgiven world; time has served its purpose;
Our Identity is found at last, which forgiveness has restored to us.

Let Your Memory Return to Me
(Inspired by ACIM Lesson 291)

Christ's vision looks through me today—
His sight shows all forgiven.
The world I see's no longer gray
When I accept His vision!

It is given us to recognize
His holiness we share,
Because we've opened up our eyes
And given up despair.

This day my mind is quiet
To hear the Thoughts you've given me;
Your Voice no longer silent,
Now I seek Your memory.

Part II

Joy Is the Only Outcome
(Inspired by ACIM Lesson 292)

Joy is the only outcome found in everything God Wills;
It's up to us when this is reached—no joy is found until
We let go of the ego's will and choose God's Will instead;
This is the Will of our true Self, the ego's will misled.

While we think this will is real, we will never find the end
He has appointed as the outcome of the problems we contend.
Yet is the ending certain, for in the end God's Will is done,
In earth and into Heaven for the truth of us is One.

Today we thank You, Father, for Your steadfast guarantee
Of only happy outcomes and our return to sanity.
You've promised a solution for every problem we perceive;
Peace and Love and happiness from You will be received.

Love Remains the Only State
(Inspired by ACIM Lesson 293)

All fear is past, its source is gone—
All its thoughts have been withdrawn.
Love remains the only state
Whose Source is here to demonstrate.

Can the world seem bright and clear
While showing me distorted fear?
Yet in the present, Love's in sight—
The world reflects its holy Light.

The world sings hymns of gratitude;
Its vision finally is renewed.
We see a world forgiven at last,
And all its sins are in the past.

Part II

The Body Is a Neutral Thing
(Inspired by ACIM Lesson 294)

The Holy Son of God I am—
Can I be something else as well?
Did God create what could be damned—
A mortal, frail, fragile shell?

What use has God's beloved Son
Have for what must die?
The body cannot be His Son—
Just a thing you occupy.

The body is a neutral thing,
When used to serve God's Will;
With Spirit's purpose it can bring
The Son's release from hell.

Its neutrality protects it
While it is occupied,
A serviceable unit
To be used and laid aside.

The Holy Spirit has a plan
Where we can be redeemed—
The spirit that appears as man
Awakens from his dream.

I Use the Eyes of Christ to See
(Inspired by ACIM Lesson 295)

Christ asks that He
May use my eyes
And thus redeem
The world from lies.
He offers peace
Of mind to me,
Dream release
And serenity.
He takes away
But every pain
On His pathway
Where Love remains.
As I am saved
From what I made,
The world is saved,
Our lilies laid.
While fear appears
In many forms—
It disappears
In Him transformed.
Christ has asked
This gift of me
That we might bask
In Unity.
I use the eyes

Part II

Of Christ to see
And visualize
Reality—
That His forgiving
Love may bless
All things
With God's own holiness.

The Holy Spirit Needs My Voice
(Inspired by ACIM Lesson 296)

The Holy Spirit needs my voice
That all may hear and now rejoice,
And hear Your Holy Word through me,
Releasing all from what can't be.

Now I would use no words but Yours,
And have no thoughts apart from Yours,
For only Your thoughts are what is true;
It's to Your Voice I listen to.

For I would save the world I made,
Where my projected guilt is laid;
As I have damned the world I see,
And now it's time to set it free.

We teach today what we would learn,
Hastening a quick return.
Our goal becomes a simple one—
The freedom of Your holy Son.

The Holy Spirit gladly aids,
Releasing from the hell we made,
When we allow Him to persuade
To seek the path that He has laid.

Part II

Salvation's Creed
(Inspired by ACIM Lesson 297)

Forgiveness is the gift I give—
It is the only gift I need,
And every time that I forgive,
The gift I give I do receive.

This is Salvation's simple creed—
The way to waken from the dream;
Salvation is my only need—
It's given me when I redeem.

How certain are the Father's ways,
Accomplished by His holy grace;
I walk to You without delays
By looking at Christ's holy face.

The outcome is completely sure,
Each step completed faithfully;
Our forgiveness has ensured
In You we reach our destiny.

Eternity with You Is Sure
(Inspired by ACIM Lesson 298)

My gratitude lets love appear,
To be accepted without fear.
Reality is now restored,
Intrusions on my sight ignored;
Forgiveness takes them all away;
The Light of Love has shined my way.
And now I draw near to the end;
Senseless journeys I transcend,
Accepting what God's given me,
Not fearing my Identity,
Knowing that I will be saved,
From all the fruitless dreams I made.

Father, I come to you today,
The path to You the only way.
You are beside me, this I know,
I'm grateful for the gifts bestowed
Of peace and certain sanctuary—
With Love that is extraordinary,
And escape from all that would obscure,
That eternity with You is sure.

Part II

My Holiness Stands Forever Perfect
(Inspired by ACIM Lesson 299)

My holiness is far beyond my ability to know,
Yet the Father that created me assures me it is so.

My holiness is not of me, it's not destroyed by sin,
Illusions can obscure it but can't dim the light within.

You can't put out its radiance nor dim its holy light,
Its blessed luminescence lights the world up very bright.

It stands forever perfect and in it all things are healed,
For they remain as You created them—their Unity is sealed.

I can know my holiness for holiness created me;
Your Will is that You will be known—Your Will is what will be.

For but an Instant Does This World Endure
(Inspired by ACIM Lesson 300)

For death and sorrow are the certain lot
Of all within the world that guilt begot.
But false perceptions cannot keep their hold—
The dark storm clouds must pass to now behold
Unclouded peace that's obvious and sure,
For but an instant does this world endure.

Father, we seek your holy Word today,
For we, Your loving Sons, have lost our way.
But finally, we've listened to Your Voice,
And Heaven certain, now we do rejoice.
Our true Identity with You is sure,
For but an instant does this world endure.

Part II

The Second Coming
(Inspired by ACIM Workbook Part II, #9)

What is Christ's Second Coming but the correction of mistakes?
It returns the mind to sanity that separation would forsake.
It is a part of the condition that restores the never-lost,
The consent to let forgiveness rest upon all things without a cost.

It's the all-inclusive nature of Christ's Second Coming that permits
It to embrace the world you see and hold you safe inside of it.
Forgiveness lights Its way because it shines on all as One,
And thus is Oneness recognized at last for every Son.

The Second Coming ends the lessons that the Holy Spirit shares,
Making way for the Last Judgement and the end of all despair.
Learning ends in one last summary that extends beyond itself,
Reaching up to God and joining all our minds with our true Self.

Its Coming is the one event which time itself can not affect,
As all who came to die are now released from their effects.
In the holy Light of God, the Sons acknowledge they are One,
All their joy has just begun, the Father smiles upon His Son.

Pray the Second Coming will be soon but do not rest—
It needs your eyes and ears and voice and all your willingness.
Let's rejoice that we can do God's Will and thereby expedite—
The Second Coming of the Christ in God's most holy Light.

Unless I Judge I Cannot Weep
(Inspired by ACIM Lesson 301)

Unless I judge, I cannot weep—
I cannot suffer pain,
Nor can I drown in water deep
Where illusions still remain.

This is my home—I judge it not;
I let it be but what You will—
The tears I shed will be forgot;
My mind is finally still.

Let me behold through happy eyes
Forgiveness has released,
From all distortion's alibis
And see a world of peace.

The world of God's a happy one;
We now add our joy to it,
And bless it with the joy we've won—
What we condemned we now acquit.

Part II

His Light Illuminates the Way
(Inspired by ACIM Lesson 302)

Our eyes are opening at last; Your holy world awaits us;
Our sight has finally been restored, our eyes no longer treasonous.

We suffered for the things we thought, forgetting we're Your Son;
Now the darkness is no longer seen for there's light to look upon.

Christ's vision changes dark to light and fear now disappears,
For love has finally come our way—Your Voice is what we hear.

Let me forgive your world today that I may understand—
Its holiness reflects my own; illusions can't withstand.

Our Love awaits us patiently as we go to Him today;
He walks beside us, and His Light illuminates the way.

Heaven's Son Is Born in Me Today.
(Inspired by ACIM Lesson 303)

Watch with me, angels, watch with me today;
The holy Christ is born in me today.
No longer can I ever be forlorn;
Be still with me while Heaven's Son is born.

Let earthly sounds be quiet, and the sights
I'm used to seeing, fade into Your Light.
Let Christ be welcomed where He is at home;
No longer can He ever be alone.

Please let Him hear the sounds He understands
And see the sights that show God's Love is grand.
Let Him no longer be a stranger here,
But born again in Spirit's stratosphere.

Your Son is welcome—He has come to save
Me from the evil self that I have made.
He is my Self as You created me,
And now I claim my true Identity.

Part II

I Can Obscure My Holy Sight
(Inspired by ACIM Lesson 304)

I can obscure my holy sight
If this is my decision;
I can't behold the face of Christ
Unless I use His vision.

Perception is a mirror—
It is not a fact to find,
And what I see is my own fear
Reflected from my mind.

I would bless the world I see
By seeing through Christ's eyes,
And know forgiveness comes to me
When His Light is recognized.

Forgiveness is salvation—
Your gift is mine to give,
That Your Son find liberation,
In all that we forgive.

The Peace of Christ Is Given to Us
(Inspired by ACIM Lesson 305)

Those who use only Christ's vision
Find a peace so deep and quiet
It undoes all your division—
Everyone should want to try it.

All the world departs in silence,
No more to be the home of fear;
The Holy Spirit's loving guidance
Leads to peace, and love appears.

The peace of Christ is given to us—
It is Your Will that we be saved;
His Loving peace has come to save us
From the judgements we have made.

Part II

We Ask for Only What You Give
(Inspired by ACIM Lesson 306)

There is nothing but Christ's vision
That can heal the division—
But will I use His sight today
If He can offer me a way
To see a world devoid of sin
Whose touch is almost like Heaven
So that an ancient memory
Can finally be returned to me?

It is today that I go past
All of the fears that I've amassed,
Restored at last to love and peace—
All of my fears have been released.
Finally, now, I am redeemed
From all the pain within my dreams,
Born anew so happily
Into a world of His mercy.

Our Father we return to You—
There's nothing here we have to do.
Remembering this very day,
We never really went away.
We come to You in gratitude,
With open hearts that are renewed;
We ask for only what You give,
That in Your holy Light we live.

The End of Conflict
(Inspired by ACIM Lesson 307)

Father, Your holy Will is mine—
There is no other will than thine.
Let me not make another will,
For it is senseless and can't fulfill,
And it will only cause me pain;
Happiness I will not gain.

If I would have but what You give,
Then in Your Light there I must live.
I must accept Your Will for me
For happiness to come to me,
Where conflict is impossible
And peace is now unstoppable.

Into a state we now succumb
Where conflict can no longer come
Because we join our will with Yours—
The holy truth of One endures.
I'm still as You created me,
And now I see our Unity.

Part II

The Time Is Now
(Inspired by ACIM Lesson 308)

I've conceived of time in such a way that I defeat my aim;
This instant is the only time there is for me to claim.

To reach past time to timelessness, I must change time's perception;
The past and future I must lose to break the mind's deception.

The only interval in which I'm saved from time is now;
Forgiveness comes to set me free, if I will just allow.

The birth of Christ is now without a future or a past;
He restores the world to timelessness and love that can't avast.

I thank You for this instant for it's now I am redeemed;
This is the instant You have set for your own Son's release.

Within Me Is Eternal Innocence
(Inspired by ACIM Lesson 309)

Within me is eternal innocence—
It is God's Will that it be there always,
And I, His Son, whose will is limitless,
Can will no change in God's Heavenly ways.

The sure denial of my Father's Will
Is not to recognize His Will is mine;
To look within is but to find my will
As God created holy and divine.

I fear to look within because I think
I made another will that is not true.
It has no *real* effects on anything—
Within me is the holiness of You.

I walk to God with lilies in my hand
And place them on the altar in my mind;
I reach to God and take my brother's hand—
One shared Identity is what I find.

Part II

This Day I Would Spend with You
(Inspired by ACIM Lesson 310)

This day, my Father, I would spend with You,
As You have chosen best for me to do,
And what I find is not of time at all,
The sweet reminder of time before the fall.

Your gracious calling to Your holy Son,
The sign Your grace bestowed on me has come,
And it's Your Will that I be free today—
Your Holy Spirit shows the world the way.

We spend together, this day just You and I—
The joy You bring no longer is denied.
The world joins with us in our thankfulness—
We are restored to peace and holiness.

Who gave salvation to us sets us free;
There is no room for fear in us to be,
For we have welcomed Love into our hearts,
And we no longer can ever be apart.

The Last Judgement
(Inspired by ACIM Workbook Part II, #10)

Christ's Second Coming gives the Son of God this holy gift—
To hear the Voice for God proclaim what's false does not exist.
What's true is true—it's never changed— It's here perception ends;
The now corrected mind that has projected all transcends—
It gives a silent blessing as perception makes a shift.

The final judgement on the world contains no condemnation—
It sees the world forgiven without sin or allegation.
Without a cause, and in Christ's sight, it merely slips away
To nothingness where it was born and where it ends its stay,
And all the figures in the dream have reached their own salvation.

You who thought the Last Judgement would condemn the world to hell—
Accept this holy truth of God—your fears He will dispel.
God's Judgement is the gift of the Correction He bestowed—
It frees you from your errors and the effects they seemed to show;
It releases all your suffering and brings happiness as well.

The Last Judgement is God's own appointed plan to bless His Son,
And calls him to return to the eternal peace they share as One.
Be not afraid of Love for it alone can heal all sorrows,
And waken you from dreams of pain and fear of your tomorrows.
Salvation bids you welcome it and let all errors be undone.

Part II

This is God's Final Judgement: You are still My holy Son,
Forever loved and innocent—We never were not One.
You're as limitless as God Himself and still forever pure,
Completely changeless, forever loving, and always now secure.
Awaken and return to Me— you're My beloved Son.

Father, We Let Your Love Decide
(Inspired by ACIM Lesson 311)

Judgement is a weapon used by you to hide what's true;
It separates you from your Self with each unholy view.
Now seen apart, it makes of it what you would have it be,
And therefore judges falsely as it can't see totality.

We will not use judgement today, but offer it to Him,
Who has a different use for it—His Judgements won't bedim.
He will relieve us of the agony of the judgements we have made
Against ourselves and brothers as the price that we have paid.

We wait with open minds to hear Your Judgement of Your Son,
And reestablish peace of mind by finding we are One.
We use the Holy Spirit's eyes to see what He would see,
And so we let Your Love decide just what Your Son must be.

Part II

I Choose to See No Separation
(Inspired by ACIM Lesson 312)

The world seen through the body's eyes
Was projected from the mind
That believed in separation's lies
From the terror it did find.

The guilt was so enormous
That it could not be contained;
It was projected into orbit,
But the guilt inside remains.

Now the splintered mind can see
The guilt in someone else;
It need not be a part of me
If I don't see it in myself.

So now I see the guilt in you—
You are the evil one,
Believing in the body's view
From you I must now run.

If I choose to see your body,
Then I must be a body too;
The perception of the body
Means the separation's true.

But if I choose to see it
Through the Holy Spirit's eyes,
Then I perceive only the spirit
And disregard the body's lies.

Spirit can't be separated
No matter what you see—
The spirit God created
Still shares One Identity.

Today I set the world free
From the judgements I have made;
This is Your only Will for me—
Our innocence is saved.

Part II

Sin Is Forgiven in His Holy Vision
(Inspired by ACIM Lesson 313)

In Him there is a vision
That beholds all things forgiven;
Fear is gone with every sin,
And love has been
Invited in.
And now love will come in
Wherever it is asked in;
The gift of His Vision
Is our true perception.
In His sight that is given
Are all things forgiven,
Now I may awaken
From my dark illusion
And look deep within
To see there's no sin.
Today we envision
In Christ's holy vision
The right of rescission
Of all our division.
This day it is given
To all that may listen
Of our joint decision
To see the Son risen.

We Use the Present to Be Free
(Inspired by ACIM Lesson 314)

Looking at the world from our newly acquired perception,
There comes a future that is very different from the past.
The future is now recognized as only an extension
Of the present that's been freed from fears that we've amassed.

Past mistakes can cast no shadows on this new perception;
Fear has lost its idols and being formless has no effects.
Death can't claim the future now for life is its intention,
And all the needed means are now provided and protect.

Who can grieve or suffer when the present has been freed
Extending its security into a future filled with joy?
We choose to lose the past and use the present to be free,
Secure now in Your Love we follow the Guide that You employ.

Part II

Now Our Spirits Are Aligned
(Inspired by ACIM Lesson 315)

A thousand treasures come to me
With every moment that would be;
I'm blessed with gifts throughout the day,
Of value I cannot convey.
My heart is gladdened when my brother
Can now smile upon another,
And speak a word of gratitude
In Spirit's loving attitude.

My mind receives these gifts I'm shown
And takes them as they are its own,
And all who find the way to God
Become my savior to applaud,
Pointing out the way to me
And giving me His certainty
That what he learned is surely mine
As now our spirits are aligned.

Every Gift I Give Belongs to Me
(Inspired by ACIM Lesson 316)

As every gift my brothers give is mine,
So every gift I give belongs to me,
No shadow's left upon my holy mind—
And now His grace is given unto me.

My treasure house is full without a cost,
And angels now watch over it for me,
Assuring not a single gift is lost,
As only more are added there to see.

For I would come to where my treasures be,
And enter where I truly am at home,
Among the gifts that God has given me,
Where past is gone, and I am made welcome.

Father, I would accept Your gifts today;
I trust in You who will provide the means
By which I can behold without delay—
The value of Your gifts can now be seen.

Part II

Where You Lead Is Where I Want to go
(Inspired by ACIM Lesson 317)

I have a special place to fill—
A role for me alone,
And now salvation waits until
I make this part my own.

Until I choose to make this choice,
I am the slave of time;
My spirit now cannot rejoice
As human destiny is mine.

But when I willingly adhere
To the plan God has for me,
I see salvation's already here
For my brothers and for me.

Father, it's You I want to know,
And where You lead me to
Is where I want to go.
What You'd have me do, I do.

Your way is always certain,
And the end is but secure;
It's time to lift the curtain
To see the light that's been obscured.

In You All Parts Are Reconciled
(Inspired by ACIM Lesson 318)

How could there be a single part
That stands alone or could impart
A value on God's holy Son
That is not shared with everyone?

Salvation's purpose is to find
The sinlessness placed in the mind
Of ourselves and all we see—
The means and end are inside me.

I accept Atonement for myself;
We stand as One in our true Self.
My mind no longer is defiled—
In You all parts are reconciled.

Part II

My True Self Shares Its Totality
(Inspired by ACIM Lesson 319)

When all arrogance has been removed
And only truth remains,
The mind has finally been renewed—
Freed from the ego's chains.

The ego thinks that what one gains
Totality must lose;
The Will of God says what one gains
Is given all to use.

What goal but the world's salvation
Could You have given me?
My true Self has no limitation—
It shares totality.

The Son of God Is Limitless

(Inspired by ACIM Lesson 320)

The Son of God is limitless—
Because His power's given us;
There are no limits on his might,
His peace, his joy, his holy sight.

His holy Will can't be denied—
His Father shines upon his mind,
And lays before it everything—
The strength and Love that Heaven brings.

It's *me* to all that this is given—
The power of God's holy Vision.
It's me the Holy Spirit guides;
In me the Father's Will abides.

Your Will can do all things in me
And extends to all the world through me.
There is no limit on Your Will
That is given to me to fulfill.

Part II

Creation
(Inspired by ACIM Workbook Part II, # 11)

Creation is the aggregate of all the Father's Thoughts;
There was no time when all that He created there was not.
Nor can anything that He created suffer harm—
God's Thoughts remain exactly as they were and as they are.

God's Thoughts are given all the power that the Father holds,
For He would add to Love by its extension that unfolds.
What God has willed to be forever One will still be One—
It cannot change and stays the same when thoughts of time are done.

Creation is the opposite of all illusions that you see;
Creation is the holy Son of God in God's glory.
Its Oneness is forever held within His holy Will,
Beyond all risk of harm or sin or any spot of ill.

While we seem to be discrete, unaware of Unity,
Beyond our doubts, and past all fears, there still is certainty.
For Love remains with all its Thoughts, its sureness being theirs;
God's memory is in our minds—its Oneness still is there.

Let our function only be to let His memory return,
And let God's Will be done on earth while in this brief sojourn.
Our Father gently calls to us—we hear His holy Voice;
Our minds returned to sanity, and in Him we rejoice.

My Freedom Lies in God
(Inspired by ACIM Lesson 321)

I did not understand what made me free;
I did not know what freedom really is,
But now I hear Your Voice directing me;
There's nothing that I choose to hear but this.

For now I trust in You who's given me
Eternal freedom as Your holy Son.
At last, the way to You is clear to me—
My freedom lies in You, and You alone.

It is my will that I return to You;
How happy am I to have found my way.
The ego's lies we now can see right through;
The world's salvation can be ours today.

The glory of Your Son forever free,
No longer lost, but Yours eternally.

Part II

The Only Thing I Lose Is Fear
(Inspired by ACIM Lesson 322)

I sacrifice illusions that play out inside my mind,
And as illusions go, it is Your gifts that I now find.
Awaiting me in welcome and in readiness to give,
His memory abides in every gift I get from Him,
And every dream serves only to conceal my true Self,
Which is the holy Son of God in the likeness of Himself.

To God, all sacrifice remains forever inconceivable;
I sacrifice only in dreams that seem to be believable.
As You created me, I give up nothing that You gave me,
And what you did not give to me does not contain reality.
What loss can I anticipate except the loss of fear
With the restoration of my mind by letting Love appear?

You Must Sacrifice Your Suffering
(Inspired by ACIM Lesson 323)

Here is the only sacrifice
The Father asks of you—
For you to live in paradise
You must give up what isn't true.

You're asked to give up suffering
And every sense of loss,
The sadness separation brings—
Get off the rugged cross!

You must give up anxiety
And every form of doubt,
To let His loving memory
Finally come about.

We pay the debt we owe to truth,
Letting go of self-deceptions,
Joy becomes our only truth
As we accept correction.

This sacrifice You ask of me
Is one I gladly make;
The returning of Your memory—
The mind is now awake.

No longer can we be deceived—
Fear is gone, and with it, pain;
Peace has finally been received,
And only Love remains.

Part II

We Follow One Who Knows the Way
(Inspired by ACIM Lesson 324)

Father, You are the One Who gave
The plan for my salvation.
The way You set on the path You pave
Will lead to celebration.

And if I wander off a while,
I cannot lose my way;
Your loving Voice will reconcile
The path that led astray.

My brothers all can follow me
As I lead them now to You;
It's Your Voice that does direct me
Where to go and what to do.

We needn't tarry and cannot stray
But an instant from His Hand;
We follow One Who Knows the way
And guarantees things go as planned.

God's Ideas Reflect the Truth
(Inspired by ACIM Lesson 325)

The world I see before me reflects a process in my mind;
The mind makes up an image of what it wants and seeks to find.
These images are projected outward and looked upon as real;
From the minds own insane wishes an insane world is now revealed,
And from its judgement comes a world condemned without appeal.

Yet its only from forgiving thoughts a gentle world comes forth,
With mercy for the holy Son and a kindly home and hearth,
A place where he can rest a while before he journeys on,
And help his brothers walk with him on the road that leads to God.

Father, Your ideas reflect the truth—the world's not what it seems;
Let me behold what Yours reflect, as mine but make up dreams.

Part II

I Am Forever Your Effect
(Inspired by ACIM Lesson 326)

In Your Mind I was created,
In Your Love Illuminated;
A Thought that never left its Source—
There was never a divorce.
I am forever Your Effect,
A difference you cannot detect.
And you forever are my Cause,
And like Yourself, I have no flaws.
As You created me, I stay,
A perfect state without decay.
For where You put me, I abide,
With all Your attributes inside.
It is Your Will to have a Son,
Cause and Effects are still as One.
Because I am but His Effect,
I have His power if I elect
To let Him share His Will with me—
This is how it's s'posed to be.
Your plan is what I follow here,
And when I do, there is no fear.
And as I near the end I know—
Heaven is where I want to go,
Just resting in tranquility,
Enveloped in Your Unity.
Now we see the world transformed,

Now forgiven, it's reformed,
And so we let it disappear,
And into God we reappear.

Part II

I Just Call Out Your Name
(Inspired by ACIM Lesson 327)

God promised He would hear my call
And give an answer too;
If I've learned anything at all,
Then I know that this is true.

Faith in Him will come to me—
It's this faith that will endure,
For He has not abandoned me—
Of this, I now am sure.

He patiently awaits my call,
To give all the help I need,
And if I accidentally fall,
To Him, His Voice will lead.

Your promises will never fail
If I but test them out;
Let me try them and avail,
And therefore judge them not.

Your Word is always One with You—
You give the means whereby
Conviction comes and surety too,
That in Your Love I do abide.

Another Will's Preposterous
(Inspired by ACIM Lesson 328)

The world is but a battleground
And all we see is upside down,
Until we listen to His Voice
And learn to make another choice.

It seems we'll gain autonomy—
Believing in dichotomy,
By seeking separation
From the rest of God's creation.

We believe this brings salvation
In the sand of its foundation;
All we find here is but sickness,
Suffering, loss, and weakness.

This is not the Father's Will for us—
Another will's preposterous!
We join with His to find our own,
And since our will is His, we're shown.

There is nothing I imagine
In my dreams that seem to sadden—
That can replace reality
Of what You would have me be.

It is Your Will I be protected—
Disunity will be corrected;
He shares His holy Will with me
For now and all eternity.

Part II

For Only Your Truth Is True
(Inspired by ACIM Lesson 329)

I thought I wandered from Your Will,
Defied it, broke its laws,
And interposed a second will
More powerful than Yours.

In truth, I am only Your Will—
Extended and extending;
This I am—it is so still—
For Your truth is never-ending.

Father, the truth of You is One,
So I am One with You.
This truth can never be undone,
And only Your truth is true.

This I chose in my creation—
Where my will was One with Yours,
Forever—You are my causation,
And so my will is Yours.

This choice was made for eternity—
It cannot be opposed,
For we share in One Identity—
It's Your Will that it be so.

I Choose Not to Hurt Myself Today
(Inspired by ACIM Lesson 330)

Let us this day accept forgiveness as our only function,
And not rely on the ego's sight and all of its disruption.
Why attack our minds and give them images of pain?
God holds His power out to us, with Love that does sustain.

The mind that is made willing to accept His holy gifts
Has been restored to spirit and extends its joy from it.
For it shares the holy Will of God united with its own;
Freed from its container, it no longer is alone.

The Self which God created cannot sin and cannot suffer;
We choose this One Identity and claim all it has to offer.
It frees us from all errors, and of this you can be sure,
That our minds have now been saved from all the lies we thought we were.

Part II

The Ego
(Inspired by ACIM Workbook Part II, #12)

The ego is idolatry, the sign of limitation—
A body doomed to suffer and die in its need for separation.
It is this "will" that sees the Will of God as enemy,
And takes a form where it's denied, without indemnity.
The ego is the proof that strength is weak, and love is fearful,
And what opposes God is what is true—its life is tearful.

The ego stands apart from All, beyond the Everywhere,
Separate from the Infinite, living out its own nightmare.
It believes it's triumphed over God and "sees" His Will destroyed,
And lives in terror of retribution which now it must avoid.
It sees external enemies that will attack and hurt him,
And to ensure security, he must attack before them.

The Son of God is egoless, what can he know of madness—
Of sorrow and of suffering when all he knows is gladness?
There is no fear of punishment, of hatred or attack—
For there is only endless peace, abundance without lack.
It's here there's never been a sin; it's always conflict-free,
Undisturbed, eternal joy, in God's tranquility.

To ever know reality, look past the ego's thoughts—
Its acts, its laws, its dreams, its hopes, and all that guilt has brought.
In suffering, the price for faith's so huge that crucifixion
Of the Son is offered in its daily benediction.
Yet just one lily of forgiveness changes darkness into light,
Returning peace unto his mind and restoring his true sight.

The Will of God Is One
(Inspired by ACIM Lesson 331)

Could the Son be so deceived, that he could actually believe
He could cause his own disease and then be left without release?

And make a plan for his damnation, by his inner condemnation—
Left in a sea of desolation, without hope of his salvation?

Could Love have left Itself? Can you have conflict with your Self?
Could the Will of God Himself not be fulfilled within His Self?

For the ego's mad collusion was just the minds delusion—
And in the mind's confusion it spawned only an illusion.

Death and all affliction are the ego's dark depiction
Of a will that's in confliction and awaiting benediction.

The forgiveness of His Son must be shared with everyone,
For *the Will of God is One between the Father and His Son.*

Part II

Forgiveness Sets Us Free
(Inspired by ACIM Lesson 332)

The ego makes illusions;
The truth shines them away.
One leads to a solution;
One leads to disarray.

The truth can never make attack—
The truth merely is;
Within it there's no place for lack—
It's where His presence is.

The mind's recalled from fantasies,
Awaking to what's real;
Forgiveness shows this world to me,
And allows the mind to heal.

Without it is the mind in chains,
Drowning in futility.
Forgiveness does dispel the rain,
And brings tranquility.

We would not bind the world today;
Fear holds it prisoner;
We allow the chains to fall away—
Our freedom now is sure.

The Name Remains the Same
(Inspired by ACIM Lesson 333)

Conflict must be abated
For it cannot be evaded—
Left in darkness, set aside,
First disguised and then denied,
And now It's seen but somewhere else,
In a self that's not your Self,
Or called by any other name—
For the name remains the same.
It can't be hidden by deceit—
If escape is what you seek,
For your mind to become clean,
As it is, it must be seen
In its given reality,
Exactly where it's thought to be,
With the purpose that the mind
Accorded it for you to find.
For only then are its defenses
Lifted from the consequences,
Allowing truth to shine on fear,
And in its light, fear disappears.
Forgiveness is the light You chose
To shine away and now dispose
Of all conflict and every doubt
The mind would pick to come about.
No light but this can end the dream

Part II

And save the world from what it seems,
For this alone will never fail
As in Your Love we will prevail.

I Receive Forgiveness by Giving Forgiveness
(Inspired by ACIM Lesson 334)

I will not wait another day
To find the treasures He has laid
On the ground ahead of me—
The door to God's reality.

For my illusions are all vain—
I let them go with every pain,
Woven out of thoughts that rest
On false perceptions by request.

God's Voice is offering the peace
Of God to me with fear's release,
To all who choose to follow Him,
And find His Light He placed within.

Today, I seek but the eternal,
Releasing me from dreams infernal;
I offer everyone forgiveness,
Beholding only sinlessness.

Part II

Forgiveness Is a Choice I Make
(Inspired by ACIM Lesson 335)

I never see my brother truly,
For that is far beyond perception;
What I see is what I wish to see—
Only the mind's conception.

To see him through the body's eyes
And behold him full of sin,
His spirit I don't recognize—
I miss the light within.

And now his sin I seem to see
That stands in him alone—
My mind now sees inside of me
And claims it as my own.

But if I choose to see Christ's face
By choosing true forgiveness,
Both of our sins are now erased—
The mind perceives us sinless.

Forgiveness is a choice I make
For no one but myself;
The sleeping mind is now awake
When it sees its One-True-Self.

Love Will Open up the Door
(Inspired by ACIM Lesson 336)

There's an altar that is hidden that perceives all things forgiven;
There was never any sin—here peace of mind can be restored.
Forgiveness sweeps away distortions of the ego mind's extortions,
Shining light into each portion that the lilies would restore—
The dwelling place of God Himself the spirit's looking for—
    And Love will open up the door.

Part II

My Sinlessness Ensures Me Perfect Peace
(Inspired by ACIM Lesson 337)

My sinlessness ensures me perfect peace;
All thoughts of lack and loss have been released.
I've been relieved from all my suffering,
And happiness and joy are everything.

What must I do to know all this is mine?
I must accept Atonement for all time.
For God has done all things that need be done;
I need now but accept that we are One.

The Father knows exactly who I am;
The Love of God is true and cannot damn.
I must accept Atonement for myself,
And that's the way I know my own true Self.

Your Thoughts Lead Me to Salvation
(Inspired by ACIM Lesson 338)

Nothing but my thoughts affect me;
Nothing but my thoughts can scare me.
Nothing exists outside of me;
Nothing external can hurt me.

Thoughts that hurt, I now can change—
Each fearful thought can be exchanged
For happy thoughts of love and joy,
By giving up thoughts that destroy.

I may still have some thoughts that frighten—
Until I learn Your Thoughts enlighten.
Your Thoughts lead me to my salvation,
To joy and love and celebration.

Part II

Let's Spend the Day in Fearlessness
(Inspired by ACIM Lesson 339)

No one desires suffering to have and hold and treasure,
But the guilty mind can think what brings it pain is really pleasure.

No one would ever willingly avoid his happiness,
But he can think that joy is pain, fearful and dangerous.

For he can be confused indeed about his want of things,
As he's asked for what will frighten him and bring him suffering.

If happiness and joy we want, let's ask for only this—
And spend the day in fearlessness, hearing just the Voice that's His.

Our Suffering Is Done
(Inspired by ACIM Lesson 340)

Father, I thank You for today;
Today is but a holy day—
It is the day Your Son's redeemed,
From illusions he has dreamed.

Today, his suffering is done;
His celebration has begun,
For finally he has heard Your Voice—
Today's the day we all rejoice.

His mind's been freed from suffering
From the light forgiveness brings.
The Son's released from what he made;
His execution has been stayed.

Be glad, be glad, be glad today!
For there's only joy and thanks this day!
Salvation is for everyone—
The Father has redeemed His Son.

Part II

Miracles Fall Like Drops of Rain
(Inspired by ACIM Workbook Part II, #13)

A miracle does not create, nor really change at all;
It looks at devastation, and shows what's seen is false.
It undoes the error in the mind within the mind's perception
And stays within time's limits while it offers a correction.
It paves the way for timelessness and Love's awakening,
For fear must slip away under the remedy it brings.

A miracle contains the gift of grace for everyone,
For the gift of grace is given and then received as One.
It illustrates the law of truth the world does not obey,
Because the world does fail entirely to understand its ways.
A miracle inverts perception which was upside down before—
The mind's now open to the truth and forgiveness is the door.

Forgiveness houses miracles and the eyes of Christ bestow
On all they look upon in love where sin has been let go.
Perception stands corrected, in His most holy sight,
That what was meant to curse has now been seen in its true light.
A miracle of love is shared with each lily of forgiveness,
And laid upon His altar now with joy and happiness.

The miracle must rest on faith because to ask for it implies
The mind has been made ready to give up the ego's lies.
Faith will bring its witnesses to what the ego can't conceive,
And let you glimpse reality where sin can't be believed.
The miracle will justify your faith and now prepare
You to see a world redeemed from what you thought was there.

Miracles Fall Like Drops of Rain

Miracles fall like drops of rain where starving creatures come to die,
The dry and dusty world's now green and we no longer cry.
The water now is plentiful, and we soar above the sky;
We share His immortality—what's born of Him can't die.

Part II

Holy Is the Father's Son
(Inspired by ACIM Lesson 341)

Holy is the Father's Son—
He is the one You smile on
With love and tenderness so dear
That in it we can defeat fear.

How pure and safe indeed are we—
We share in His Identity.
Abiding in Your holy smile,
Relaxed in love, we'll stay a while.

With all Your Love bestowed on us,
Sharing in Your One purpose,
Hand in hand in brotherhood,
Complete now in Your Fatherhood.

We won't attack our sinlessness—
It holds the Word of God for us.
We see our brother's innocence;
We share in One Magnificence.

We are His Thoughts inside Himself,
And in Him we will know our Self.
It is in His most kind reflection,
That we are saved by our election.

The Key Is in My Hand
(Inspired by ACIM Lesson 342)

I thank you, Heavenly Father, for giving me the means,
To save me from the hell I made by living inside dreams.

The key is in my hand, and I have reached the final door;
Beyond it lies the end of dreams where illusions are no more.

The veil has been lifted, and I stand before Your gate,
Wondering if I should enter, or if I'd better wait.

Let me not wait again today; let me forgive all that I see,
Allowing Your Creation to be as you would have it be.

Let me remember I'm Your Son and open up the door;
Your memory's returned to me—my mind has been restored.

And now I grab my brother's hand and bring him home with me;
We share in Your Creation, and Your Love is all we see.

Part II

Paradise Was Never Lost
(Inspired by ACIM Lesson 343)

It is the end of suffering,
And only Love remains;
For His gift of everything
Can only be to gain.

The Father only lives to give—
He never takes away,
And so, I too, elect to give,
So what I have will stay.

The Son can make no sacrifice,
For He must be complete—
Completion is the asking price;
What's whole we can't deplete.

The peace of God is always free;
Salvation has no cost.
The gift I give I give to me—
Paradise was never lost.

Today I Learn the Law of Love
(Inspired by ACIM Lesson 344)

Today, I learn the law of love, that what I give is mine;
This is the law my Father wrote—it stands the law of time.
I thought to save what I desired for myself alone,
And looked upon the treasures I collected as my own,
And found an empty space where nothing was nor ever will be—
For who can share a dream—what can illusions offer me?

Yet he whom I forgive will give me gifts beyond the worth
Of anything I've ever seen here on this planet Earth.
Let my forgiven brothers fill my store with Heaven's treasures;
Thus is the law of love fulfilled with wealth we cannot measure.
How close we are to ending this whole dream of separation,
The redemption of the Son of God with the ego's abdication.

Part II

We Offer Only Miracles Today
(Inspired by ACIM Lesson 345)

A miracle reflects Your gifts to me,
And every one I give returns to me.
The world I seem to see only deceives;
A miracle solves problems I perceive.

The miracle is closer to Your gifts
Than any other gift that I can give,
Then let me give this gift alone today—
From true forgiveness, it will light the way.

The miracle reflects His holy Light,
To bless a tired world with His true Sight.
The world we see will find its rest this day;
We offer only miracles today.

The Laws of Love Are All I Find
(Inspired by ACIM Lesson 346)

Miracles are my election,
By allowing a correction,
Of the ego mind's perception,
For the spirit's resurrection.

I will not seek the things of time—
I seek a brand-new paradigm,
And transcend all the laws of time,
By basking in Your Love, sublime.

The laws of Love are all I find;
The laws of time have slipped behind.
Your peace extended to mankind;
Your memory is in my mind.

And when the evening comes today,
And every fear has gone away,
We know now that your Love will stay;
We seek that now without delay.

Part II

I Cast My Hate to the Wind
(Inspired by ACIM Lesson 347)

Judgement is the weapon
I would use against myself;
I cannot learn my lessons
Or know the truth of my true Self.

My judgements keep my mind locked
On something that's not there;
They keep Your holy Light blocked
From being seen everywhere.

I do not know what is my will
For I've made another one,
And this one thinks attack fulfills—
It cannot see Your Son.

But You have offered freedom,
And I claim Your gift today;
I give my judgement to the One
Whose Vision knows the way.

He sees what I behold
And yet He knows what's really true.
Illusions He does not uphold—
He gives a different view.

He shows me what my dreams would hide;
He knows they are not real.
He gives the miracles that guide,
And awareness that will heal.

Miracles Fall Like Drops of Rain

I let Him judge all things today;
I let Him speak for me;
I let my fears be cast away,
And miracles I see.

Part II

Everlasting Love Surrounds Me
(Inspired by ACIM Lesson 348)

Everlasting Love surrounds me;
The peace of God is all around me.
There is no fear; there's no distress;
There's not a single spot of darkness
That's left upon the world to see.

You share with me Your perfect safety;
Your grace restores my sanity.
My mind is full of happiness
And Everlasting Love.

Alone no more, I cannot be—
The Light of Love is all I see.
I stand in perfect sinlessness,
Created in Your holiness.
I have no needs for You surround me—
In Everlasting Love.

Today I Give Up Judgement
(Inspired by ACIM Lesson349)

Today I give up judgement and use the Holy Spirit's Vision
To liberate the things I see by seeing all forgiven.
I use the law of Love to give what I would find and keep;
For every miracle I give, another one I reap.

Father, Your holy gifts are mine, and each one that I accept
Gives me a miracle to give and love to interject.
You give us grace to meet our needs and miracles to bless;
Our minds are healed by Your Love as we allow forgiveness.

Part II

Spirit Is the Truth of Me
(Inspired by ACIM Lesson 350)

Miracles reflect God's Love—
What we forgive, we are part of;
Our perception of our self
Is now attuned to our true Self.

Spirit is the truth of me—
The body's not reality;
My thoughts affect but what I see,
But cannot change the truth of me.

Father, I would turn to You—
Forgiveness will restore my view;
Your memory returns to me
In the joy of Love's reality.

Who I Am
(Inspired by ACIM Workbook Part II, #14)

I am God's Son, complete and whole, in His Love's reflection;
I am His One Creation blessed—I share in His perfection.
I am the home of God Himself—I'm where His Love resides;
I am His holy sinlessness—in my purity, His Own abides.

In these final days, our use for words is almost done;
We found a single purpose that we shared with everyone.
The truth of what we are is not for words to say or speak,
Yet we can realize our function if we live the words we speak.

We are the saviors of the world, and through our joint forgiveness
Is the world redeemed from sin, and this, our gift, is given us.
We look on all as brothers and perceive them with His Sight,
Knowing knowledge will return when we have welcomed in the Light.

We use the eyes of Christ to see a world that's now redeemed
From every single thought of sin the world has ever dreamed.
Ours are the ears that hear the Voice for God proclaim us sinless;
Our minds now joined, we bless the world and celebrate our Oneness.

We are His holy messengers—we bring His holy Word;
Our minds are changed about our aim, and we seek now but to serve.
Heaven's gate's now open and with our brothers by our side,
We walk into the Heart of God and disappear inside.

Part II

I Make a Choice to See Only What Is True.
(Inspired by ACIM Lesson 351)

My sinless brother is my guide to peace—
To see him sinless leads to my release.
My sinful brother is my guide to pain—
To see him sinful keeps my mind in chains.

My brother can't be separate from me—
The truth of spirit's shared Identity.
If he's not sinless, neither can I be;
For then we're bodies, guilty as can be.

I make a choice to see but what is true—
Our sinlessness—the Holy Spirit's view.
Our way home now is safe and very clear—
Perceive the truth and let His Love appear.

From Judgement Comes All Sorrow
(Inspired by ACIM Lesson 352)

From judgement comes all sorrow,
Without hope of joy tomorrow;
It binds my eyes and makes me blind—
Your peace and Love I cannot find.

Love, reflected in forgiveness,
Judges not, but sees all sinless;
It leads only to redemption
By adjusting the perception.

You've not left me without comfort,
For within's the Voice of support.
His Vision leads to peace that's true,
And to the memory of You.

Part II

My Identity Is Restored in Christ
(Inspired by ACIM Lesson 353)

My eyes I give to Christ today that He might help me see
That I have just one purpose and only One Identity.
His vision lights the world with love, restoring what I see,
And shows me that my brother was never separate from me.

My voice I give to Christ today that He might help me say
The perfect words to someone else that brightens up their day.
His voice of love and kindness that my brother takes away
Is without a trace of judgment as forgiveness lights the way.

My feet I give to Christ today—I bring Him where I go—
To bring joy to the weary and to lift those feeling low.
We bless the world with miracles; through us His love does flow;
In Christ is my Identity and the Love of God I know.

I Am the Christ in Me
(Inspired by ACIM Lesson 354)

I have no self except the Christ;
I have no purpose but His own.
I need not make a sacrifice
To claim what still is known.

I am beyond the reach of time
And free of earthly laws;
I need not fight for what is mine—
I am still as I always was.

For who is Christ except Your Son—
As You created him to be;
What we are is still as One—
I am the Christ in me.

It's You I Choose Today
(Inspired by ACIM Lesson 355)

I will not wait on joy today
For He's promised this to me,
Very simple is the way
To claim my Identity.
I will not stay in exile
While my treasure waits for me,
For His Love can only reconcile
My own insanity.
I need not wait an instant more
To be at peace forever,
Before me is an open door
That I can choose whenever
I agree to give up pain
And the suffering I find,
To let His peace forever reign
Inside my splintered mind.
It's You I choose; it's You I choose;
It's You I choose today,
And the only thing I lose
Is the pain that's gone away.
I am your Son, and I choose to know
My Father and Creator;
I do not have but far to go—
My mind's the liberator.

Sickness Is a Name for Sin
(Inspired by ACIM Lesson 356)

Sickness is a name for sin—
Sin is separation;
Your Name replaces thoughts of sin
With thoughts of realization.

Healing is a name for God—
He shares His Name with you.
Can perfection become flawed?
The truth you must review.

You promised You would never fail
To answer any call;
It does not matter what seems to ail
Or how hard the rain does fall.

The miracle reflects Your Love,
And thus it answers true;
Your Name replaces sin thought of
With the memory of You.

Your Name gives answer to Your Son,
Because to call Your Name—
Is merely to call his own,
For the name is still the same.

Part II

Behold His Sinlessness and You Are Healed
(Inspired by ACIM Lesson 357)

Forgiveness, truth's reflection
Is the only true correction;
It offers miracles by election
To escape prison's selection.
At this crucial intersection,
And after careful introspection,
There's no longer a projection
Of the mind's own misdirection.

Your holy Son is shown to me,
First in my brother, then in me.
Your Voice instructs me patiently
To use Your Vision so I may see
And hear Your Voice instructing me
In glorious simplicity—
Behold the sinlessness in he,
And healing you've allowed to be.

Let Me Remember
(Inspired by ACIM Lesson 358)

Let me remember my One Identity
Let me remember the holiness of me
Let me remember all I do not know
Let me remember where I want to go
Let me remember the Voice for God Himself
Let me remember the truth of my own Self
Let me remember all Your Love and care
Let me remember You are always there
Let me remember my awareness as Your Son
Let me remember the truth of us is One
Let me remember the truth of Us
Let me remember the Truth
Let me remember
Let me know
The Truth
Is One
One

Part II

The Answer is Some Form of Peace
(Inspired by ACIM Lesson 359)

God's answer is
Some form of peace—
Every pain is
Now released.
All misery
Is set aside,
The prison doors
Are open wide.
All sin you see
Is understood
As merely
Misunderstood.
All the mistakes
That we have made
Could not disgrace—
Have not waylaid.
The Son is still
But innocent,
Peace is His Will,
His one intent.
Impossible is
Every sin,
And on this
All is forgiven.
Help us forgive

For we choose peace,
Help us forgive—
We seek release.

Part II

In Holiness Do We Remain
(Inspired by ACIM Lesson 360)

It is Your peace that I would give—
I find it now when I forgive.
I remember that I am Your Son;
I see Your Light in everyone.

I'm just as You created me—
Your Light burns bright inside of me,
Undisturbed in purity,
Extending into eternity.

In holiness, we do remain;
Our sinlessness we do retain.
We share Your peace with all and then—
With this thought we say, "Amen."

We Can Never Be Apart
(Inspired by ACIM Lessons 361-365)

This holy instant I would give to You;
I choose the way that leads me to Your door.
With certainty, I follow only You;
The gifts You give, I could not ask for more.

Your Voice I hear, in charge at my request;
We walk together—fear is left behind.
Your thoughts I use—I see the world as blessed;
Your Light and Love Illuminate my mind.

I have no worries for my path is sure;
No longer do I ever walk alone,
And if the road seems rocky You insure
Your Light within me points the way to home.

You are the Voice of Love inside my heart,
And We can never ever be apart.

Part II

Homeward Bound
(Inspired by ACIM Workbook Epilogue)

Not the end, but the beginning—you can never be alone;
Your Friend goes with you every inning, for you are but His own.
He has the answer for each problem and will gladly share with you;
You need but ask it of Him and see the world through His Own View.

Your safe arrival home is certain, and your pathway now is sure,
So follow now His Voice as It's the Voice of God and yours.
His Voice speaks to you of freedom, and He knows just what you need,
For God has called you to Him, and His Voice will not mislead.

No more lessons are assigned for there's no more need of them.
Seek only for the Voice for God and listen but to Him.
He will direct your efforts, and He will direct your mind;
His is the Word that God has given to you now to find.

And now I place you in His hands with Him as your One Guide,
Through every tribulation on the road where darkness hides.
Let Him prepare you further, for now He's earned your trust;
Your walk with Him is certain—your safe arrival is a must.

You will be told exactly what it is God wills for you—
Every time there is a choice to make, He'll tell you what to do.
And so we walk with Him—from this time on, He leads the way;
Homeward bound, with peace and joy, we reach His Own doorway.

In certainty we trust our ways to Him and say, "Amen."
In peace we will continue while we trust all things to Him.
He shows us how to see the world and how to love God's Son—
His angels hover all around, reminding us we're One.

Part II

Thank You!

The Voice for God, the Voice of Jesus,
The Voice Blake called "Poetic Genius,"
I thank this Voice, in gratitude—
The Voice of Love that God imbued.
His Voice is in my mind to stay
For it Illuminates the way.
It's up ahead and just behind,
It stays forever in my mind.
It's always there to lift me up,
Past clouds of darkness to the top.
It is the Light that's always there,
Within, without and everywhere,
Where perfect Love is all around
And Oneness is what will be found.

About the author

Sandi Christie is the author of *Lilies of Forgiveness—A Course in Miracles in Haiku*. She has been a student of *A Course in Miracles* since the mid 1990's, and is an advocate of the teachings of Kenneth Wapnick, Ph.D.

www.ingramcontent.com/pod-product-compliance
Lightning Source LLC
Chambersburg PA
CBHW072143100526
44589CB00015B/2065